AF442927

Wilmshurst's
The Meaning of Masonry

by W. L. Wilmshurst
Edited and Foreword by
Michael R. Poll

Cornerstone Book Publishers
Hot Springs Village, AR
2024

Wilmshurst's The Meaning of Masonry
by W. L. Wilmshurst
Edited and Foreword by Michael R. Poll

A Cornerstone Book
Published by Cornerstone Book Publishers

Copyright © 2013, 2020 & 2024 by Cornerstone Book Publishers

Cornerstone Book Publishers
Hot Springs Village, AR
www.cornerstonepublishers.com

First Cornerstone Edition - 2013
Second Cornerstone Edition - 2020
Third Cornerstone Edition - 2024

Table of Contents

Introduction
The Position and Possibilities of the Masonic Order

THE papers collected in this book are written for members of the Masonic Order, constituted under the United Grand Lodge of England. They are offered to all in the best spirit of fraternity and goodwill and with the wish to render the Order some small return for the profit the author has received from his association with it extending over thirty-two years. They have been written to promote a deeper understanding of the meaning of Masonry, to provide an explanation that one constantly hears called for, and becomes all the more necessary given the unprecedented increase of interest in and membership of the Order at the present day.

The meaning of Masonry, however, is a subject usually left entirely unexplained and largely unrealized by its members, save for such few as making it their private study. The authorities of what in all other respects is an elaborately organized and admirably controlled community have hitherto made no provision for explaining and teaching the "noble science" that Masonry proclaims itself to be and was undoubtedly designed to impart. It seems taken for granted that reception into the Order will automatically be accompanied by an ability to appreciate all that one finds. The contrary is the case, for Masonry is a veiled and cryptic expression of the obscure science of spiritual life. The understanding of it calls for special and informed guidance on the one hand and, on the other, a genuine and earnest desire for knowledge and no small capacity for spiritual perception on the part of those seeking to be instructed. Not infrequently, one finds Brethren discontinuing their interest or membership because they find that Masonry means nothing to them and that no explanation or guidance is offered. Were such instruction provided, assimilated, and responded to, the life of the Order would be enormously quickened and deepened. Its efficiency as a means of Initiation intensified. At the same time, the fact would prove an added safeguard against the admission into the Order of unsuitable members. This is meant to be understood as not merely persons who fail to satisfy conventional qualifications but also those who, while fitted in these respects, are as yet either so intellectually or spiritually lacking as to be incapable of benefiting from Initiation in its true sense even after passing formally through Initiation rites. Spiritual quality rather than numbers is needed. The ability to understand the Masonic system and apply its implications to a personal experience rather than the unthinking conferment of its rites is needed in the Craft today.

These papers have been compiled to repair the absence of explanation. The first two have often been read as lectures at lodge meetings. Many requests that they should be printed and made more widely available led to my expanding their subject matter into greater detail than could be used for occasional lectures. Accordingly, they are amplified by containing fuller remarks on Craft symbolism. To complete the consideration of the Craft system, it was necessary to add a chapter upon that which forms the crown and culmination of the Craft Degrees, without which they would be imperfect—the Order of the Royal Arch. Lastly, a chapter has been added upon the important subject that forms the background of the rest—the relationship of modern Masonry to the Ancient Mysteries, from which it is the direct, though greatly diminished, spiritual descendant.

Thus, in five papers, I have sought to provide a survey of the whole Masonic subject as expressed by the Craft and Arch Degrees. It is hoped they illuminate the increasing number of Brethren who feel that Freemasonry enshrines something more profound and greater than they have been able to realize in the absence of guidance. It does not profess to be more than an elementary and far from exhaustive survey; the subject might be treated much more fully, in more technical terminology and with abundant references to authorities, were one compiling a more ambitious and scholarly treatise. But to the average Mason, such a treatise would prove less serviceable than a summary expressed in as simple and untechnical terms as may be and unburdened by numerous literary references. Due to the papers having been written at different times, some repetition may be found in later chapters of points already dealt with in previous ones. However, the restatement may be advantageous in emphasizing those points and maintaining the continuity of the exposition. For reasons that will be explained, the Holy Royal Arch may prove difficult to comprehend by those unversed in the literature and psychology of religious mysticism; if so, the reading of it may be deferred. But since a survey of the Masonic system would be incomplete without reference to that degree, and since it deals with matters of advanced psychological and spiritual experience—which an explanation is always difficult—the subject has been treated here with as much simplicity as possible. The goal is not to show the great heights of spiritual attainment the Craft Degrees point, but to attempt to explain them in a manner that readers will readily comprehend without some measure of mystical experience and perhaps unfamiliar with the lectures of the mystics.

Purposely, these papers avoid dealing with matters of Craft history and merely antiquarian or archeological interest. Dates, particulars of Masonic constitutions, historical changes, and developments in the external aspects of the Craft, references to old lodges, and the names of outstanding people connected therewith—these and such like matters can be read about elsewhere. They are all subordinate to what is in the moment vital and what so many brethren are hungering for— knowledge of the spiritual purpose and lineage of the Order and the present-day value of Rites of Initiation.

In giving these pages to publication, care has been taken to observe due discretion concerning essential matters. However, the Masonic system's general nature is widely known to outsiders and readily ascertainable from many printed sources. At the same time, the significant interest in and output of literature on mystical religion and the science of the inward life during the last few years has familiarized many with a subject of which, as shown in these papers, Masonry is a specialized form. To explain Masonry in general outline is, therefore, not to divulge a subject that is entirely exclusive to its members but merely to show that Masonry stands in line with other doctrinal systems teaching the same principles and to which no secrecy attaches and that it is a specialized and highly effective method of teaching those principles. Whether expressed in Masonry or otherwise, truth is always an open secret. Still, it is a pillar of light to those able to receive and profit from it and to all others one of darkness and unintelligibility. An elementary and formal secrecy is vital as a practical precaution against the intrusion of improper persons and for preventing profanation. In other respects, the essential secrets of life, and any system expounding life, protect themselves even though shouted from the housetops. This is because they mean nothing to those yet unqualified for the knowledge and unready to identify themselves with it by incorporating it into their habitual thought and conduct.

Given the great spread and popularity of Masonry today — when there are some three thousand lodges in Great Britain alone — it is also important to consider its present bearings and tendencies and consider future possibilities. The Order is a semi-secret, semi-public institution, secret regarding its activities *intra mœnia*, but otherwise of full public notoriety. Its doors are open to any applicant for admission with good character and reputation. Those who enter it, as the majority do, are entirely ignorant of what they will find there. Usually, they enter because they have Masonic friends or know Masonry to be an institution devoted to high ideals and benevolence. They may know that it can, sometimes, be socially desirable to be connected. They may be attracted to and benefit from what is disclosed to them, yet may not see anything beyond the bare form of the symbol or hear anything beyond the mere letter of the word. Their admission is quite a lottery; their Initiation too often remains a formality, not an actual awakening into an Order and quality of life previously inexperienced. Unless such an awakening eventually ensues from the careful study and faithful practice of the Order's teaching, their membership has little, if any, greater influence upon them than would ensue from their joining a purely social club.

For "Initiation" — which so many candidates have little thought of what is implied by what they ask — what does it mean and intend? It means a new beginning, a break-away from an old method and order of life, and the entrance upon a new one of larger self-knowledge, deepened understanding, and intensified virtue. It means transitioning from the merely natural state and standards of life towards a regenerate and super-natural state and standard. It means turning away from pursuing the popular ideals of the outer world, in the conviction that those ideals are but shadows, images, and temporal substitutions for the eternal Reality that underlies them. It means to discover the keen and unchangeable quest of that Reality itself and the recovery of those genuine secrets of our being that lie buried and hidden at "the center" or innermost part of our souls. It means the awakening of those yet dormant higher faculties of the soul which endue their possessor with "Light" in the form of new enhanced consciousness and enlarged perceptive faculty. And lastly, in words with which every Mason is familiar, it means that the postulant will henceforth dedicate and devote his life to the Divine rather than to his own or any other service so that by the principles of the Order, he may be better enabled to display that beauty of Godliness which, perhaps, has not before manifested through him.

To comply with this definition of Initiation, it might be helpful to test not only those who seek admission into the Order but also those who are already within it. Special qualifications of mind and intention are essential if a candidate is to benefit from the Order in the way that its doctrine contemplates. It is not necessarily the ordinary man of the world or personal friend—good fellow though he is according to usual social standards—who is either properly prepared for or likely to benefit in any vital sense by reception into it. The true candidate must indeed be, as the word *candidus* implies, a "bright white or shining, unstained man," unstained within as symbolically he is white-vestured without, so that no inward stain may obstruct the dawn within his soul of that Light which he professes to be the predominant wish of his heart on asking for admission. If he is truly desirous of learning the secrets and mysteries of his own being, he must be prepared to divest himself of all past preconceptions and thought habits with childlike humility and obedience. He will surrender his mind to the reception of some perhaps novel and unexpected truths which Initiation can impart, and which will more and more unfold and justify themselves within those, and only those, who are, and continue to keep themselves, properly prepared for them. "Know thyself!" was the injunction inscribed over the portals of ancient temples of Initiation, for with that knowledge was promised the knowledge of all secrets and all mysteries. And Masonry was designed to teach self-knowledge. But self-knowledge involves knowledge that is much deeper, vaster, and more complex than is popularly conceived. It is not to be acquired by the formal passage through three or four degrees in as many months. It is a knowledge impossible to fully achieve until ideas of every other kind have been laid aside, and a difficult path of lifelong and strenuously pursued study leads its followers to attain that knowledge. The wisest and most advanced of us is perhaps still but an Entered Apprentice at this knowledge, however high his titular rank. Here and there may be one worthy of being hailed as a Fellow-Craft in the true sense. The full Master-Mason — the just man made perfect who has actually traveled the entire path, endured all its tests and ordeals, and become raised into conscious union with the Author and Giver of Life and able to mediate and impart that life to others — is at all times hard to find.

So high, so ideal an attainment, it may be urged, is beyond our reach. We are but ordinary men in a world sufficiently occupied already with our primary civic, social, and family obligations. We are following the obvious typical path of natural life! Granted. Nevertheless, modern Speculative Masonry was instituted to point to that attainment as possible to us and as our destiny, to instill that labor of self-perfecting to those who care and dare to follow it. And to emphasize that fact, these papers are devoted. Masonry means this, or it means nothing worth the serious pursuit of thoughtful men. It is nothing that cannot be pursued outside the Craft as well as within it. It proclaims the fact that there exists a higher and more secret path of life than that which we normally tread, and that when the outer world and its pursuits and rewards lose their attractiveness for us and prove insufficient to our deeper needs, as sooner or later they will, we are compelled to turn back upon ourselves, to seek and knock at the door of a world within. It is upon this inner world, and the path to and through it, that Masonry promises light, charts the way, and indicates the qualifications and conditions of progress. This is the sole aim and intention of Masonry. Behind its more elementary and obvious symbolism, behind its counsels to virtue and conventional morality, there exists the framework of a scheme of initiation into that higher path of life where alone the secrets and mysteries of our being are to be learned. A scheme moreover that, as will be shown later in these pages, reproduces for the modern world the main features of the Ancient

Mysteries, and a learned writer on the subject has well described that as "an epitome or reflection at a far distance of the once universal science."

However, because Masonry has meant less than this for a long time and for many, it has yet to fulfill its original purpose of being the efficient initiating instrument it was designed to be. Its energies have been diverted from its true instructional purpose into social and philanthropic channels, which are excellent in their way but foreign to and additions upon the primal main intention. Indeed, so little perceived or appreciated is that central intention that one frequently hears it confessed by men of eminent position in the Craft that only their interest in its great charitable institutions keeps their connection with the Order alive. Relief is a duty incumbent upon a Mason, but its Masonic interpretation is not meant to be limited to physical necessities. The spiritually as well as the financially poor and distressed are always with us, and Masonry was designed to minister to the former, equally as to the latter. Theoretically, upon reception into the Craft, every man acknowledges himself as within the category of the spiritually poor. The initiate is content to renounce all temporal riches if, by that sacrifice, his hungry heart may be filled with those good things that money cannot purchase.

But if Masonry has yet to fulfill its primary purpose and, though engaged in admirable secondary activities, is yet an initiating instrument of low efficiency, it may be that, with a better understanding of its designs, that efficiency may become considerably increased. During the last two centuries, the Craft has gradually developed from small and crude beginnings into its present vast and highly elaborate organization. Today, the number of lodges and craft memberships is increasing beyond all precedents. One asks oneself what this growing interest portends and what it will, or can be made to, lead. The growth synchronizes with a corresponding defection of interest in orthodox religion and public worship. It need not now be enquired whether or to what extent the simple principles of faith and the humanitarian ideals of Masonry are with some men taking the place of the theology offered in the various Churches. It is probable that, to some extent, they do so. However, the fact is that the ideals of the Masonic Order make a wide appeal to the best instincts of large numbers of men, and the Order has gradually become the greatest social institution in the world. Its principles of faith and ethics are simple and of virtually universal acceptance. Providing means for the expression of universal fraternity under a common Divine Fatherhood and common loyalty to the headship and established government of the State, it leaves room for divergences of private belief and view upon matters upon which unity is impracticable and perhaps undesirable. It is utterly clean of politics and political intrigue.

Nevertheless, it has unconsciously become a real, though hidden, asset of political value, both in stabilizing the social fabric and tending to foster international amity. The elaborateness of its organization, the care and admirable control of its affairs by its higher authorities are praiseworthy in the extreme. While in the conduct of its lodges, there has been and is a progressive endeavor to raise the standard of ceremonial work to a far higher degree of reverence and intelligence than was perhaps possible under conditions existing not long ago. The Masonic Craft has grown to dimensions undreamed of by its founders, and, at its present rate of increase, its potential and influence in the future are quite invaluable.

What now needs to intensify the worth and usefulness of this great Brotherhood is to deepen its understanding of its own system and educate its members on its rites and philosophy's deeper meaning and true purpose. Were this achieved, the Masonic Order would become, in proportion to that achievement, a spiritual force of monumental importance to the world. Carried to its fullest, that achievement would involve the revival, in a form adapted to modern conditions, of the ancient Wisdom-teaching and the practice of those Mysteries that became proscribed fifteen centuries ago but of which modern Masonry is the direct and representative descendant, as will appear later in these pages.

The future development and the value of the Order as a moral force in society depend, therefore, upon the view its members take of their system. If they do not spiritualize it, they will increasingly materialize it. If they fail to interpret its veiled purport, to enter the understanding of its underlying philosophy, and to translate its symbolism into what is signified thereby, they will be mistaking shadow for substance, a husk for the kernel, and secularizing what was designed as a means of spiritual instruction and grace. It is from a lack of instruction rather than a desire to learn the meaning of Masonry that the Craft suffers today. But, as one finds everywhere that desire exists, and so, for what they may be worth, these papers are offered to the Craft as a contribution towards satisfying it.

Let me conclude with an apology and an aspiration.

In the *Chronicles* of Israel, it may be read that after long preparatory labor, after employing the choicest material and the most skillful artificers, Solomon the King finally ended building and beautifying his Temple. He dedicated it to the service of the Most High that work of his hands was in a state as perfect as human provision could make it. And how that then, but not till then, his offering was accepted, and the acceptance was signified by a Divine descent upon it so that the glory of the Lord shone through and filled the whole Temple.

So — if we will have it, may it be with the Temple of the Masonic Order. Since Speculative Masonry's inception, it has been building and expanding over the last three hundred years, fashioning living stones into a far-reaching organic structure. Freemasonry was brought gradually, under the good guidance of its rulers, to high perfection on its temporal side. With respect to its external observances, it was made available for high purposes and gave godly witness in a dark and troubled world. Upon these preliminary efforts, let there now be invoked this crowning and completing blessing — that the Spirit of Wisdom and Understanding may descend upon the work of our hands in abundant measure, prospering it still farther and filling and transfiguring our whole Masonic Temple.

W.L.W.
1922

Foreword to the Cornerstone Edition
Do We Really Need This Book?

WHY do Masons need a book like *The Meaning of Masonry* 100 years after publication? Can we actually benefit from this book? Why can't we just go to meetings and enjoy ourselves? Can't we support our lodges and help those in need through our charities? Well, this book will provide thoughts as to why this is just not possible. Let's look at a story, a fable. Maybe it will remind you of someone in your lodge. Maybe it will remind you … of you.

Not long ago, a young man turned in his petition to a Masonic lodge. Maybe a relative of his was a Mason, or perhaps he learned of Freemasonry from a popular book or movie. Regardless, he expressed his desire to join.

A few weeks after turning in his petition, he received a phone call from a man who told him he was a member of the investigation committee working on his petition. He asked the young man if he and two other lodge members could come to his house and meet with him. They met at the appointed time. It was a good meeting. Questions were asked, and everyone learned a bit more about each other.

The committee told the young man that Freemasonry is not an insurance agency. Masonry does not extend health benefits or promise financial assistance. While lodges and individual Freemasons have a long and honorable history of assisting those in need, Freemasonry is not designed to be a charitable organization like the Red Cross.

Freemasonry is also not a civic association such as the Jaycees or Lions Club. Its primary goal is to take good men and, through moral instruction, give them the keys to hopefully improve their lives.

The young man absorbed all the information he was given. He then inquired about the origins of Freemasonry. He was informed that our beginnings are not fully known or clear.

We acknowledge our antiquity; he said that most Masons date Masonry back to around 1717 with the establishment of the Grand Lodge of England. However, many assert that our roots extend much further — to the era of the old Operative Freemasons. Some even argue that our philosophy and method of symbolic education can be traced back even far earlier. Regrettably, we lack definitive answers. The young petitioner accepted this, and the committee departed. Both sides were satisfied.

The young man was quietly excited. He understood that what he was about to join was something ancient and significant. He couldn't put into words why he felt this way, but he felt it in his heart. He had done his research. He had already delved into popular books and conducted online searches concerning Freemasonry. He was wise enough to disregard the plethora of sensationalism surrounding Freemasonry. He dismissed the wild superhero/Jedi claims and baseless satanic accusations. But he recognized that there was something unique about Freemasonry, its method of instruction through degrees, and the entire Masonic philosophy. He felt good about his decision to join.

In a few weeks, a letter came in the mail telling him that the lodge had voted on his petition. The ballot was clear, and the date of the initiation was set. But there were many questions that he had forgotten to ask. One thing that he was unsure about was how he should dress for the initiation. He thought about calling but then remembered some of the books he owned and how the Masons wore business suits, and some even wore tuxedoes. The photos were not all that old, so he thought he should try to match their dress. He knew this was something special but assumed they would have told him if they wanted him to wear a tux. So, he decided to wear his suit.

When he showed up at the lodge, a number of the members were wearing old blue jeans and equally faded and worn polo shirts — some were T-shirts. Others looked like they were wearing soiled work clothes and had come directly to the lodge from work. He felt a bit out of place in such a casual atmosphere. One of the men laughed when he saw him and asked if he was going to church or a wedding.

The young man waited downstairs and was finally called up for the initiation. He felt slightly uncomfortable as the man who came down for him laughed and said loudly, "Now, you are in for it!" In for what? What did he mean by that?

A kindly, elderly man placed him in a little room and seemed sincerely interested in his well-being. This made him feel better. The degree began.

After the degree ended, the young man had mixed emotions. He knew what he had experienced was important, but why was there so much laughter and talking going on? Why did he hear a considerable amount of yelling out instructions? Clearly, some who spoke did not know their lines (they were stumbling and fumbling over every few words), and others, from everywhere, were telling the officers what to say (and loudly).

While walking around, he also heard about someone's wife being sick and another's cousin building a new garage. What did all that have to do with his degree? But, afterward, everyone was so friendly. Maybe he expected too much. Maybe Freemasonry is just a group of men who occasionally meet to enjoy themselves and try to do antiquated and meaningless rituals.

The young man's feelings about Masonry changed from before his joining. These were all nice guys. Every time he went to a meeting, he was greeted with smiles, friendly handshakes, and inquiries about his health and well-being.

There was a mixture of blue-collar workers and professional men. All seemed truly interested in the lodge, but most could not answer even the most basic questions concerning Freemasonry. It was almost as if Freemasonry and the lodge were two completely different things.

Queries about the ritual or history were always directed to one brother, called the 'answer man.' They were a pleasant group of men — friends — but there was nothing extraordinary in the lodge; nothing like the way he perceived Masonry before he became a member. This was a club comprised of good men who would gather a few times a month to enjoy themselves. They would socialize and share a few laughs during a pleasant evening. That seemed to be the extent of his expectations from the lodge experience. The books, however, seemed to be alluding to something more. But what? Who were the Freemasons that he had read about? Did they ever exist? Or was it all a fabrication to sell books?

After a few months, the young man found that a TV show was scheduled at the same time as his lodge meeting. It was a show that he had wanted to watch for some time. He chose the show over the lodge. Over the next few months and years, choosing many events over the lodge meetings became easier and easier.

Eventually, the young man attended the lodge maybe once or twice a year. He tried to attend some of the important meetings, but he did so out of a feeling of obligation, not enjoyment. He did see some who truly seemed to enjoy every meeting. These were the men who kept the lodge alive.

At a few meetings, some who were always there gently scolded him for not attending more lodge functions. "You know, the lodge depends on its members, and if you don't support the lodge, it will fail." But what was he to do? Was he morally obligated to continually go to a place that provided him with no benefit other than a few laughs and a meal? He had tried, but after months of only hearing a reading of the last meeting, bills that needed to be paid, who was sick, and discussion of the next planned social event, he grew disinterested. He knew that he could spend his time in more productive ways.

So, was he to be blamed as was suggested? He even read such things from "ranking" Masons who seemed to put all responsibility for the success or failure of a body on his simply attending, regardless of what was offered. The man at the top was never to blame; and even if he was, nothing was ever done. There was no accountability for poor leadership. It was always the rank-and-file members who seemed to be the responsible parties.

The suggestion was that the young Mason was lacking something, and he needed to "wake up" and give his total support to whatever was offered.

Was there a lack in him?

Freemasonry either failed this young man in about every way possible, or there indeed was some lacking in him, or maybe he misunderstood the actual nature of Masonry. Is Freemasonry only a club of good men who try to do charitable work and hold friendly meetings, or is it an organization designed to educate and elevate its members through moral instruction?

In several publications, the young man saw written: "Freemasonry is the world's oldest and largest fraternity. Its history and tradition date to antiquity. Its singular purpose is to make good men better."

OK, that's clear. But how do we do that?

Since this quote was written in a Masonic education publication, maybe that should give us a clue. We should teach and instruct our candidates. There are countless books and articles written on Masonic education. We learn the importance of education and teaching in our very ritual. But, apart from the ritual, do we actually *teach* Freemasonry, or is it only words to be spoken or read and not acted upon? How many young men are lost to us simply because we fail to do what we say we will do?

William Lowe Bryan (the 10th president of Indiana University) is credited with writing: "Education is one of the few things a person is willing to pay for and not get." This is sometimes true (and has been for many years) regarding Freemasonry. The hole left when quality education ceased in the lodges was replaced with additional fellowship. That's not a bad thing, but it's not Freemasonry's lifeblood. Initiation and making good men "better" are our main reasons for existence. But what does it mean?

Wilmshurst's The Meaning of Masonry is a book that Masons should read … but really, they should not focus on the words. They should focus on how they feel when reading it. It is a book that will reach those who can most benefit from it. It can open unforeseen, unknown doors. There is more to Freemasonry than our meetings, lodge rooms, officers, ritual, and aprons. This book may be exactly what you need to understand the true meaning of Masonry. Personally, I find it of great value.

Michael R. Poll
2020

Wilmshurst's
The Meaning of Masonry

CHAPTER I.
The Deeper Symbolism of Freemasonry

A CANDIDATE proposing to enter Freemasonry has seldom formed any definite idea of what he is joining. Even after admission, he usually remains quite at a loss to explain satisfactorily what Masonry is and for what purpose his Order exists. He finds that it is "a system of morality veiled in allegory and illustrated by symbols," but that explanation, while true, is partial and does not fully enlighten him. For many members of the Craft, to be a Mason implies merely a connection with a body that seems to combine the natures of a club and a benefit society. They find, of course, a certain religious element in it. Still, as they are told that religious discussion, which means, of course, sectarian religious discussion, is forbidden in the lodge. They may infer that Masonry is not a religious institution and that its teachings are intended to be merely secondary and supplemental to any religious tenets they may happen to hold. One sometimes hears it remarked that Masonry is "not a religion," which is quite true, but sometimes it is a secondary or supplementary religion, which is quite untrue. Again, Masonry is often considered, even by its members, to be a system of extreme antiquity that was practiced and has come down in nearly its present form from Egyptian or at least from early Hebrew sources: a view which again possesses the merest fraction of truth. In brief, the vaguest notions about the origin and history of the Craft are obtained. At the same time, the still more fundamental subject of its immediate and present purpose and its possibilities remains almost entirely outside the consciousness of many of its members. We meet in our lodges regularly; we perform our ceremonial work and repeat our instructions/lectures night after night, and there our work ends — as though the ability to properly perform this work were the *be-all* and the *end-all* of Masonic work. Seldom (or never) do we employ our lodge meetings for that purpose for which, quite as much as for ceremonial purposes, they were intended, *viz.*: for "expatiating on the mysteries of the Craft." Perhaps our neglect to do so is because we have imperfectly realized what those mysteries were when our Order was introduced to us.

Yet, there are many brethren who would willingly repair this apparent deficiency. Masonry profoundly appeals to and calls out to them, even in its more limited aspect. They feel that their membership in the Craft is a privilege that has brought them into the presence of something greater than they know, that enshrines a purpose, and that could unfold a message deeper than they at present realize.

In a brief address like this, attempting to deal adequately with what I have suggested is hopeless. We need improvement in our knowledge of the system to which we belong. The most one can hope to do is offer a few hints or clues, which those who desire may develop for themselves in the privacy of their thoughts. In the last resource, no one can communicate the deeper aspects of Masonry to another. Every man must discover and learn them for himself, although a friend or Brother may be able to conduct him a certain distance on the path of understanding. We know that even the elementary and superficial secrets of the Order must not be communicated to unqualified persons. The reason for this injunction is not so much because those secrets have any special value but because that silence is intended to be typical of that which applies to the greater, deeper secrets, some of which, for appropriate reasons, must not be communicated, and some of which indeed are not communicable at all, because they transcend the power of communication.

It is well to emphasize then, at the outset, that Masonry is a sacramental system, possessing, like all sacraments, an outward and visible side consisting of its ceremonial, its doctrine, and its symbols which we can see and hear, and an inward, intellectual, and spiritual side. A side concealed behind the ceremonial, doctrine, and symbols, and available only to the Mason who has learned to use his spiritual imagination and can appreciate the reality behind the veil of an outward symbol. Anyone, of course, can understand the simpler meaning of our symbols, especially with the help of the explanatory lectures, but he may still miss the meaning of the scheme as a necessary whole. It is absurd to think that a vast organization like Masonry was ordained merely to teach grown-up men of the world the symbolical meaning of a few simple builders' tools or to impress upon us such elementary virtues as temperance and justice. The children in every community school are taught such things. Nor was Masonry created to enforce such simple principles of morals as brotherly love, which every church and every religion teaches; or as relief, which is practiced quite as much by non-Masons as by us; or of truth, which every infant learns upon its mother's knee. There is surely, too, no need for us to join a secret society to be taught that the Volume of the Sacred Law is a fountain of truth and instruction or to go through the great and elaborate ceremony of the third degree merely to learn that we all die. The Craft whose work we are taught to honor with the name of a "science," a "royal art," surely has some larger end in view than merely teaching the practice of social virtues common to all the world and by no means the monopoly of Freemasons. Certainly, it behooves us to acquaint ourselves with what that larger end consists of, to enquire why the fulfillment of that purpose is worthy of being called a *science*, and to ascertain what *are* those *mysteries* to which our doctrine promises we may ultimately attain if we apply ourselves assiduously enough to understanding what Masonry is capable of teaching us.

Realizing what Masonry is not, let us ask what it is. But before answering that question, let me give you certain facts that will enable you to appreciate the answer better. In all periods of the world's history, and every part of the globe, secret orders and societies have existed outside the limits of the official churches to teach what is called "the Mysteries." These groups existed to impart to suitable and prepared minds certain truths of human life, certain instructions about divine things, about human nature and human destiny, which was undesirable to publish to the multitude who would corrupt those teachings and apply the esoteric knowledge communicated to perverse and perhaps to disastrous ends.

These Mysteries were formerly taught, we are told, "on the highest hills and in the lowest valleys," which is merely a figure of speech for saying, first, that they have been taught in circumstances of the greatest seclusion and secrecy, and secondly, that they have been trained in both advanced and simple forms according to the understanding of their disciples. It is, of course, common knowledge that great secret systems of the Mysteries (referred to in our lectures as "noble orders of architecture," *i.e.*, of soul-building) existed in the East, in Chaldea, Assyria, Egypt, Greece, Italy, among the Hebrews, among Mahommedans, and Christians they are to be found. All the great teachers of humanity, Socrates, Plato, Pythagoras, Moses, Aristotle, Virgil, the author of the Homeric poems, and the great Greek tragedians, along with St. John, St. Paul, and innumerable other great names, were initiates of the Sacred Mysteries. The *form* of the teaching communicated has varied considerably from age to age; it has been expressed under different veils, but since the ultimate truth, the Mysteries aim at teaching is always the same, there has always been taught, and can only be taught the same doctrine. What that doctrine was, and still is, we will consider presently so far as we can speak of it and as Masonry expresses it. For now, let me merely say that behind all the official religious systems of the world and all the great moral movements and developments in the history of humanity have stood what St. Paul called the keepers or "stewards of the Mysteries." From that source, Christianity itself came into the world. From them originated the great school of Kabalism, that marvelous system of secret, oral tradition of the Hebrews, a strong element of which has been introduced into our Masonic system. They also issued many fraternities and Orders, such as the great Orders of Chivalry and the Rosicrucians, as well as the school of spiritual alchemy. Lastly, they introduced Speculative Freemasonry in the seventeenth century.

To trace the genesis of the movement, which came into activity some 300 years ago (our rituals and ceremonies having been compiled around the year 1700), is beyond the purpose of my present remarks. It may merely be stated that the movement incorporated the slender ritual and the elementary symbolism that, for centuries previously, had been employed in connection with the medieval Building Guilds. Still, it gave them a far fuller meaning and wider scope. It has always been customary for trade guilds, and even modern societies, to spiritualize their trades and make the tools of their trade point to simple moral lessons. No trade lends itself more readily to such treatment than the builder's. Still, wherever a great industry has flourished, you will find traces of that industry becoming allegorized and of the allegory being employed for the simple moral instruction of operative members of the industry. I am acquainted, for instance, with an Egyptian ceremonial system, some 5,000 years old, which taught precisely the same things as Masonry but in terms of shipbuilding rather than architecture. However, the terms of architecture were employed by those who originated modern Masonry. They were used in Masonry because they were in use among certain trade guilds then in existence, and lastly, because they were highly effective and significant from the symbolic point of view.

All that I wish to emphasize at this stage is that our present system is not one coming from remote antiquity: that there is no direct continuity between us and the Egyptians, or even those ancient Hebrews who built, in the reign of King Solomon, a certain Temple at Jerusalem. The spiritual doctrine concealed within the architectural phraseology is extremely ancient in Freemasonry. This doctrine is an elementary form of the doctrine taught to all ages, regardless of its expressed garb. Our teachings, for instance, recognize Pythagoras as having undergone numerous initiations in different parts of the world and as having attained great eminence in science. Certainly, Pythagoras was not a Mason in our present sense. Still, it is also perfectly true that Pythagoras was an advanced master in the knowledge of the Secret Schools of the Mysteries. It is those paths of wisdom that some small portion of is enshrined in our Masonic system.

What was the purpose the creators of our Masonic system had in mind when they compiled it? To this question, you will find no satisfying answer in ordinary Masonic books. Indeed, nothing is drearier and more dismal than some Masonic literature and history. They are often devoted to considering unessential matters relating to the external development of the Craft and its ancient aspects. They fail to deal with its central meaning and essence. It's a failure that sometimes may be intentional but more often seems due to a lack of knowledge and awareness. In too many cases, the true inner history of Masonry has not been given, not even to the Craft itself. There are members of the Craft to whom it is familiar and who, in due time, may feel justified in gradually making public some portion of what is known in interior circles. But until that time comes, and that the Craft itself may better appreciate what can be told, it is desirable, even necessary, that its members should make some personal effort to realize the meaning of their own institution. They should view Freemasonry less as a merely pleasant social order and more as a sacred and serious method of initiation into the profoundest truths of life. It remains with the Craft itself to determine its future. The Craft shall enter its full heritage, or by failing to realize and to safeguard the value of what it possesses, it will become corrupted and pass into disrepute and deserved oblivion, as has been the fate of many secret Orders in the past.

There are signs, however, of a nearly universal increase of interest, of a genuine desire for knowledge of the spiritual content of our Masonic system. I am glad to be able to offer to my brethren some light and imperfect outline of what I consider to be the true purpose of our work. A study of this which may deepen their interest in the work of the Order and make Masonry for them a living, profound reality, rather than a mere pleasurable appendage to social life.

To state things briefly, Masonry offers us, in dramatic form and using dramatic ceremonies, a philosophy of the spiritual life of man and a diagram of the process of regeneration. We shall see presently that that philosophy is not only consistent with the doctrine of every religious system taught outside the ranks of the Order but that it explains, elucidates, and more sharply defines the fundamental doctrines common to every religious system in the world, whether past or present, whether Christian or non-Christian. The world's religions, while all aim to teach truth, express that truth in different ways, and we are more prone to emphasizing differences than to look for correspondences in what they teach. In some Masonic lodges, the candidate makes his first entrance to the lodge room amid the clash of swords and the sounds of strife to suggest to him that he is leaving the confusion and jarring of the religious sects of the exterior world and is passing into a Temple wherein the brethren dwell together in unity of thought regarding the basal truths of life. These truths can permit no difference or schism.

Allied with no external religious system itself, Masonry is yet a synthesis, a concordat, for men of every race, of every creed, of every sect, and its foundation principles being common to them all. "As it was in the beginning, so it is now and ever shall be, into the ages of ages." Hence, it is that every Master of a Lodge is called upon to swear that no innovation in the body of Masonry (*i.e.*, in its substantial doctrine) is possible since it already contains a minimum, and yet a sufficiency, of truth which none may add to nor alter, and from which none may take away. Since the Order accords perfect liberty of opinion to all men, the truths it has to offer are entirely "free *to*" us according to our capacity to assimilate them. While those to whom they do not appeal, those who think they can find a more sufficing philosophy elsewhere are equally at liberty to be "free *from*" them. Men of honor will find it their duty to withdraw from the Order rather than suffer the harmony of thought to be disturbed by their presence.

The admission of every Mason into the Order is, we are taught, "an emblematical representation of the entrance of all men upon this mortal existence." Let us reflect a little upon these weighty words. To those deep, persistent questions that present themselves to every thinking mind, What am I? Whence come I? Whither do I go? Masonry offers emphatic and luminous answers. Each of us, it tells us, has come from that mystical "East," the eternal source of all light and life, and our life here is described as being spent in the "West" (that is, as far removed from those we came from and to which we are returning, as is West from East in our ordinary computation of space). Hence, every Candidate, upon admission, finds himself in a state of darkness in the West of the lodge. He is echoing symbolically the incident of his actual birth into this world, which he entered as a blind and helpless babe. In his early years, not knowing whither he was going, after many stumbling and irregular steps, after many deviations from the true path and after many tribulations and adversities incident to human life, he may finally ascend, purified and chastened by experience, to a more significant life in the eternal East. Hence, in the E.A. degree, we ask, "As a Mason, whence come you?" and the answer, coming from an apprentice (i.e., from the natural man of undeveloped knowledge) is "From the West," since he supposes that his life has originated in this world. But, in the advanced degree of M.M., the answer is that he comes "From the East," for by this time the Mason is supposed to have so enlarged his knowledge as to realize that the primal source of life is not in the "West," not in this world; that existence upon this planet is but a transitory sojourn, spent in search of "the genuine secrets," the ultimate realities, of life; and that as the spirit of man must return to God who gave it, so he is now returning from this temporary world of "substituted secrets" to that "East" from which he originally came.

As the admission of every candidate into a Lodge presupposes his prior existence in the world without the lodge, our doctrine presupposes that every soul born into this world has lived in and has come hither from an anterior state of life. It had lived elsewhere before it entered this world; it will live elsewhere when it passes; hence, human life is a parenthesis amid eternity. But upon entering this world, the soul must assume material form; in other words, it takes upon itself a physical body to enable it to enter into relations with the physical world and to perform the functions appropriate to it in this particular phase of its career. Need I say that the physical form with which we have all been invested by the Creator upon our entrance into this world, and in which we shall all divest ourselves when we leave the lodge of this life, is represented among us by our Masonic apron? This, our body of mortality, this veil of flesh and blood clothing the inner soul of us, this is the real "badge of innocence," the common "bond of friendship," with which the Great Architect has been pleased to invest us all: this, the human body, is the badge which is "older and nobler than that of any other Order in existence" and though it is a body of humiliation compared with that body of Light which is the promised inheritance of him who endures to the end, let us never forget that if we never do anything to disgrace the badge of flesh with which God has endowed each of us, that badge will never disgrace us.

Brethren, I charge you to regard your apron as one of the most precious and speaking symbols our Order has to give you. Remember that when you first wore it, it was a piece of pure white lambskin, an emblem of purity and innocence we always associate with the lamb and the newborn child. Remember that you first wore it with the flap raised, it being thus a five-cornered badge, indicating the five senses, using which we enter relations with the material world around us (our "five points of fellowship"), but also indicated by the triangular portion above, in conjunction with the quadrangular portion below, that man's nature is a combination of soul and body. The three-sided emblem at the top added to the four-sided emblem, making seven the perfect number. For, as it is written in an ancient Hebrew doctrine with which Masonry is closely allied, "God blessed and loved the number seven more than all things under His throne," by which is meant that man, the seven-fold being, is the most cherished of all the Creator's works. Hence, the lodge also has seven principal officers, and to be perfect, seven brethren are required. However, the deeper meaning of this phrase is that the individual man, in virtue of his seven-fold constitution, constitutes the "perfect lodge" if he knows himself and analyzes his nature correctly.

Since "Masonic birth," we have also been given three lesser lights by which the lodge within ourselves may be illuminated. For the "sun" symbolizes our spiritual consciousness, the higher aspirations and emotions of the soul; the "moon" betokens our reasoning or intellectual faculties, which (as the moon reflects the light of the sun) should reflect the light coming from the higher spiritual faculty and transmit it into our daily conduct. At the same time, "the Master of the Lodge" is a symbolical phrase denoting the will-power of man, which should enable him to be the master of his own life, to control his actions, and keep down the impulses of his lower nature, even as the stroke of the Master's gavel controls the lodge and calls to order and obedience the brethren under his direction. By the assistance of these lesser lights within us, a man is enabled to perceive what is, again symbolically, called the "form of the lodge," *i.e.*, how his human nature has been composed and constituted, the length, breadth, height, and depth of his being. By their help, too, he will perceive that he, his body, and his soul are "holy ground," upon which he should build the altar of his own spiritual life, an altar which he should suffer no "iron tool," no debasing habit of thought or conduct, to defile. By then, too, he will perceive how Wisdom, Strength, and Beauty have been employed by the Creator, like three grand supporting pillars, in the structure of his organism. And by these, finally, he will discern how there is a mystical "ladder of many rounds or staves," *i.e.*, that innumerable paths or methods used which men are led upwards to the spiritual Light encircling us all.

I cannot too strongly impress upon you, Brethren, that, throughout our rituals and lectures, the references made to the lodge are *not* to the building where we meet. That building is intended to be a symbol, a veil of allegory concealing something else. "Know ye not," says the great initiate St. Paul, "that ye are the temples of the Most High and that the Spirit of God dwelleth in *you*?" The real lodge referred to throughout our rituals is our personalities, and if we interpret our doctrine in the Light of this fact, we shall find that it reveals an entirely new aspect of the purpose of our Craft.

After investment with the apron, the initiate is placed in the N.E. corner. Thereby, he is invited to learn that the foundation-stone of his spiritual life was duly and truly laid and implanted within himself at his birth into this world. He is charged with developing it and creating a superstructure for it. At this stage, two paths are open to him: a path of light and one of darkness, a path of good, and one of evil. The N.E. corner is the symbolically dividing place between the two. In symbolic language, the N. always signifies the place of imperfection and lack of development; in olden times, the bodies of suicides, reprobates, and unbaptized children were always buried in the north or sunless side of a churchyard. The seat of the junior members of the Craft is allotted to the north, for, symbolically, it represents the condition of the spiritually unenlightened man. He is the novice in whom the spiritual light latent within him has not yet risen above the horizon of consciousness and dispersed the clouds of material interests and the impulses of the lower and merely sensual life. The initiate placed in the N.E. corner is intended to see, then, that on the one side of him is the path that leads to the perpetual light of the East, into which he is encouraged to proceed, and that on the other is that of spiritual obscurity and ignorance into which he can remain or relapse. It is a parable of the dual paths of life open to each one of us. On one hand, is the path of selfishness, material desires, and sensual indulgence, of intellectual blindness and moral stagnation. On the other, is the path of moral and spiritual progress, in pursuing which one may decorate and adorn the lodge within him with the ornaments and jewels of grace and with the invaluable furniture of true knowledge. It is one which he may dedicate, in all his actions, to the service of God and his fellow men. And remember that of those jewels, some are said to be moveable and transferable. This is because when displayed in our own lives and natures, their influence becomes transferred and communicated to others, which helps uplift and benefit our fellows' lives. At the same time, some jewels are immovable because they are permanently fixed and planted in the roots of our being and are the raw material entrusted to us to work out of chaos and roughness into due and true form.

The ceremony of our first degree, then, is a swift and comprehensive portrayal of the entrance of all men into physical life and spiritual life. As we extend congratulations when a child is born into the world, we also receive with acclamation the candidate for Masonry who, symbolically, is seeking spiritual rebirth. Herein, we emulate what is written of the joy that exists among the angels of heaven over every sinner who repents and turns towards the light. The first degree is also eminently the degree of preparation, self-discipline, and purification. It corresponds with that symbolical cleansing accorded in the sacrament of Baptism, which, in the churches, is the first degree in the religious life and which is administered appropriately at the font, near the entrance of the church, even as the act itself takes place at the entrance of the spiritual career. For all of us, such initial cleansing and purifying is necessary. As has been beautifully written by a fellow worker in the Craft:

"Tis scarcely true that souls come naked down
To take abode up in this earthly town,
Or naked pass, of all they wear denied.
We enter slipshod and with clothes awry,
And we take with us much that by-and-by
May prove no easy task to put aside.
Cleanse, therefore, that which round about us clings;
We pray Thee, Master, ere Thy sacred halls
We enter. Strip us of redundant things,
And meetly clothe us in pontificals. [*]

In the schools of the Mysteries, when aspirants for the higher life were wont to quit the outer world and enter temples or sanctuaries of initiation, prolonged periods were allotted to the practical achievement of what is briefly summarized in our first degree. We are told seven or more years was normal, though less in worthy cases. The most severe tests of discipline, purity, and self-balance were required before a neophyte was permitted to pass forward, and a reminiscence of these tests of fitness is preserved in our working by the conducting of the candidate to the two wardens and submitting him to a merely formal trial of efficiency. For it is impossible today, as it was impossible in ancient times, for a man to reach the heights of moral perfection and spiritual consciousness which were then, and are now, the goal and aim of all the Schools of the Mysteries and all the secret orders, without purification and trial. Complete stainlessness of body and utter purity of mind is essential to attaining things of the great and final moment. "Who," says the Psalmist (and remember that the Psalms were the sacred hymns used in the Hebrew Mysteries), "Who will go up to the hill of the Lord, and ascend to His Holy Place? Even he that hath clean hands and a pure heart"; whence it comes that we wear white gloves and aprons as emblems that purify our hearts and wash our hands in innocence. So also, our Patron Saint (St. John) teaches, "He who hath this hope in him purifies himself, even as He (*i.e.*, the Master whom he is seeking) is pure." For he who is not pure in body and mind: he who is enslaved by passions and desires, or by bondage to the material interests of this world is, by the very fact of his uncleanness, prevented from passing on. Nothing unclean or that defiles a man, we are told, can enter into the kingdom. Therefore, our candidates are advised that if they have "money or metals about them," it is to be removed. For if not and if they are subject to any attraction or mental defilement to such, their real initiation into the higher things, of which our ceremony is but a dramatic symbol, must be deferred and repeated again and again until they are cleansed and fit to pass on.

After purification comes contemplation and enlightenment, which are the special subjects of the second degree. In time, the candidate for the Mysteries, after protracted discipline and purification enabling his mind to acquire complete control over his passions and his lower physical nature, was advanced. It was done as he may advance himself today, to study his more interior faculties, to understand the science of the human soul, and to trace these faculties in their development from their elementary stage until he realizes that they connect with and terminate in the Divine itself. The secrets of his mental nature and the principles of intellectual life at this stage gradually unfolded to his view. You will thus perceive, Brethren, that the F.C. degree, sometimes regarded by us as somewhat uninteresting, typifies, in reality, a long course of personal development requiring the most profound knowledge of our nature's mental and spiritual side. It involves not merely the cleansing and control of the mind but a full comprehension of our inner constitution, the hidden mysteries of our nature, and spiritual psychology. In this degree, our attention is called to the fact that the Mason who has attained proficiency in this grade has been enabled to discover a sacred symbol placed in the center of the building, alluding to the G.G.O.T.U. Doubtless, we have often asked ourselves what that phrase and symbol imply. Need I repeat that the building alluded to is not the temple we meet in but is ourselves? The sacred symbol at the center of the roof and the floor of this outward temple is but symbolic of that which exists at the center of us and which was spoken of by the Christian Master when He proclaimed that "the kingdom of heaven is within you." At the depths of our being, concealed beneath the heavy veils of the sensual, lower nature, resides that vital and immortal principle. It is said to "allude to" the G.G. because it is nothing but a spark of God Himself inherent within us. The injunction was written over the old temples of the Mysteries: "Man, know thyself, and thou shalt know the universe and God." Happy then is the Mason who has purified and developed his nature to fully realize the meaning of the "sacred symbol" of the second degree. He has found God present not outside but within himself. But to find the "perfect points of entrance" to this secret, emphasis is woven into our teaching on the necessity of complete moral rectitude.

Here again, the symbolism of our work becomes incredibly profound and interesting. He who desires to rise to the heights of his being must first crush and abandon his lower nature and inclinations. He must journey what elsewhere is described as the way of the Cross, and that Cross is indicated by the conjunction of those working tools (which, when united, form a cross), and that "way" is involved in the moral performance of all that we know those working tools signify. By perfecting his conduct by struggling against his natural propensities, the candidate is working the rough ashlar of his nature into the perfect cube. I would also ask you to observe that the cube contains a secret; when unfolded, it denotes and takes the form of the cross.

The inward development that the second degree symbolizes is typified by lowering the triangular flap of the apron upon the rectangular portion below. This is equivalent to the rite of Confirmation in the Christian Churches. It denotes "the progress we have made in science," in other words, it indicates that the higher nature of the man, symbolized by the trinity of spirit, has descended into and is now permeating his lower nature. Hitherto, in his state of ignorance and moral blindness, the spiritual part of his nature has, as it were, but hovered above him. He has been unconscious of its presence in his constitution, but now, having realized its existence, the day-spring from on high has visited him, and the nobler part of him descends into his lower nature, illuminating and enriching it.

Now, the man who so develops himself speedily becomes more conscious of the difficulties of his task. He is more sensitive to the obstacles the life of the outer world places in the way of spiritual life. But he is taught to persist with fortitude and prudence and develop the highest within him with "fervency and zeal." He realizes that the Eternal Wisdom utilizes difficulties and obstacles placed in his way as the necessary means of developing the latent and potential good in him and that as the rough ashlar can only be squared and perfected by chipping and polishing, so he also can be made perfect only by toil and suffering. He sees that difficulty, adversity, and persecution serve a benevolent purpose. These are his "wages," and he learns to accept them "without scruple and diffidence, knowing that he is justly entitled to them, and from the confidence he has in the integrity" of that employer who has sent him into this far-off world to prepare the materials for building the temple of the heavenly city. And so, as the sign peculiar to the degree suggests, he endeavors to examine and lay bare his heart, to cast away all impurity from it. He stands, like Joshua, praying that the light of day may be extended to him until he has accomplished the overthrow of his inward enemies and every obstacle to his complete development.

The aspirant who attains proficiency in the work of self-perfecting to which the F.C. degree alludes, has passed away from the N. side of the lodge, the side of darkness and imperfection, and now stands on the S.E. side in the meridian sunlight of moral illumination. But he is still far removed from that fuller realization of himself and of the mysteries of his nature, which the spiritual adept or Master Mason can attain. Before that attainment is reached, there remains "that last and greatest trial" for him by which alone he can enter into the great consolations and make acquaintance with the supreme realities of existence. In the places where the great Mysteries have always been taught, what is ceremonially performed in our third degree is no mere symbolical representation as with us but an actual, vital experience of a most severe character. That experience is one that the nature of which can hardly be made intelligible, or even credible, to those unfamiliar with the subject. I refrain, therefore, from more than mere mention of it. Observing only that it is one not involving physical death, and in this respect, our ceremony is only in accord with the experience symbolized. If you closely follow the raising ceremony, there is only a distinct reference to the body's death. Such death symbolizes another kind of death since the candidate is eventually restored to his former worldly circumstances and material comforts. At this stage, his earthly Masonic career is not represented as coming to a close. All that has happened in the third degree is that he has symbolically passed through a great and striking change: a rebirth or regeneration of his whole nature. He has been "sown a corruptible body," but there has been raised in him "an incorruptible body," and death has been swallowed up in the victory he has attained over himself. I sometimes fear that the too conspicuous display of the emblems and trappings of mortality in our lodges is apt to create the false impression that the death to which the third degree alludes is the mere physical change that awaits all men. But a far deeper meaning is intended. The Mason who knows his science knows that the death of the body is only a natural transition of which he needs to have no dread whatever. He also knows that when the time for it arrives, that transition will be a welcome respite from the bondage of this world, from his prison-like husk of mortality, and the daily burdens incident to existence in this lower plane of life.

All he fears is that when the time comes, he may not be free from those "stains of falsehood and dishonor," those imperfections of his nature, that may delay his after-progress. No! the death to which Masonry alludes, using the analogy of bodily death and under the veil of a reference to it, is that death-in-life to a man's own lower self, which St. Paul referred to when he asserted, "I die daily." It is over the grave, not of one's dead body but of one's lower self, that the aspirant must walk before attaining the heights. What is meant is that complete self-sacrifice and self-crucifixion, which, as all religions teach, are essential before the soul can be raised in glory "from a figurative death to a reunion with the companions of its former toils" both here and in the unseen world. The perfect cube must pass through the metamorphosis of the Cross. The soul must voluntarily and consciously pass through a state of utter helplessness from which no earthly hand can rescue it. In trying to raise him from which the grip of any succoring human hand will prove but a slip until, at length, Divine Help itself descends from the Throne above and, with the "lion's grip" of almighty power, raises the faithful and regenerated soul to union with itself in an embrace of reconciliation and at-one-moment.

In all the schools of the Mysteries and the world's great religions, attaining the spiritual goal described is enacted or taught under the veil of a tragic episode analogous to our third degree. In each, there is a Master whose death the aspirant is instructed to imitate in his person. In Masonry, that prototype is Hiram Abiff, but it must be made clear that there is no historical basis for the legendary account of Hiram's death. The entire story is symbolic and was purposely invented for the symbolic purposes of our teaching. If you closely examine it, you will perceive how apparent the correspondence is between this story and the story of the death of the Christian Master related in the Gospels, and it is needless to say that the Mason who realizes the meaning of the latter will comprehend the former and the veiled allusion that is implied. In one case, the Master is crucified between the two thieves; in the other, he is killed between two villains. In one case, the penitent and the impenitent thief appear; in the other, we have the conspirators who voluntarily confess their guilt and are pardoned and the others who are found guilty and put to death. At the same time, the moral and spiritual lessons deduced from the stories correspond. Every Christian is taught that in his own life, he must imitate the life and death of Christ, so every Mason is "made to represent one of the brightest characters recorded in our annals." Still, as the annals of Masonry are contained in the volume of the Sacred Law and not elsewhere, it is easy to see who the character is who is alluded to. As that great authority and initiate of the Mysteries, St. Paul, taught, we can only attain the Master's resurrection by "being made conformable unto His death," and we "must die with Him if we are to be raised like Him." It is in virtue of that conformity, in virtue of being individually made to imitate the Grand Master in His death, that we are made worthy of certain "points of fellowship" with Him. The "five points of fellowship" of the third degree are the five wounds of Christ. The three-year ministry of the Christian Master ended with His death, and these refer to the three degrees of the Craft, which also end in the mystical death of the Masonic candidate and his subsequent raising or resurrection.

The name Hiram Abiff signifies in Hebrew "the teacher (Guru, or enlightened one) from the Father," a fact which may help you still further to recognize the concealed purpose of the teaching. Under the name of Hiram, then, and beneath a veil of allegory, we see an allusion to another Master. It is this Master, this Elder Brother, who is alluded to in our lectures, whose "character we preserve, whether absent or present." Whether He is present in our minds or not, and regarding whom we "adopt the excellent principle, silence." Lest at any time there should be any among us trained in some other than the Christian Faith, and to whom on that account the mention of the Christian Master's name might prove an offense or provoke contention.

To typify the advance by the candidate at this stage of his development, the apron assumes greater elaborateness. It is garnished with a light blue border and rosettes, indicating that a higher than the natural light now permeates his being and radiates from his person and that the wilderness of the natural man is now blossoming as the rose. In the flowers and graces incident to his regenerated nature, while upon either side of the apron are seen two columns of light descending from above, streaming into the depths of his whole being, and terminating in the seven-fold tassels which typify the seven-fold prismatic spectrum of the supernal Light. He is now lord of himself, the true Master Mason, able to govern that lodge within himself. He has passed through the three degrees of purifying and self-perfecting and squared, leveled, and harmonized his triple nature of body, soul, and spirit. On attaining Mastership, he also wears the triple *Tau*, which comprises the form of a level but is also the Hebrew form of the Cross; the three crosses upon the apron thus correspond with the three crosses of Calvary.

To sum up the importance of teaching the three degrees, it is clear that from grade to grade, the candidate is being led from an old to an entirely new quality of life. He begins his Masonic career as the natural man; he ends it by becoming, through its discipline, a regenerated, perfected man. To attain this transmutation, this metamorphosis of himself, he is taught first to purify and subdue his sensual nature. Then, he purifies and develops his mental nature. Finally, by surrendering his old life and losing his soul to save it, he rises from the dead a Master. He is a just man made perfect, with larger consciousness and faculties, an efficient instrument for use by the Great Architect in His plan of rebuilding the Temple of fallen humanity, and capable of initiating and advancing other men to participate in the same great work.

The evolution of man into a champion was always the purpose of the ancient Mysteries. The real purpose of modern Masonry is *not* the social and charitable purposes to which so much attention is paid but the expediting of the spiritual evolution of those who aspire to perfect their nature and transform it into a more perfected quality. This is a definite science, a royal art, which we can practice. Joining the Craft for any purpose other than studying and pursuing this science is to misunderstand its meaning. Hence, no one should apply to enter Masonry unless from the deepest promptings of his own heart, as it hungers for Light upon the problem of its nature. We are all imperfect beings, conscious of something lacking in us that would make us what, in our best moments, we hope will be. What is that which is lacking in us? "What is that which is lost?" And the answer is "The genuine secrets of a Master Mason," the proper knowledge of ourselves, the conscious realization of our divine potentialities.

The essence of the Masonic doctrine is that all men in this world are searching for something in their nature that they have lost but may hope to find with proper instruction and by their patience and industry. Its philosophy implies that this temporal world is the antipode of another and more real world from which we originally came. It is a world where we may accelerate our return through self-knowledge and self-discipline as our teaching inculcates. This implies that this world is where symbolic stones and timber are being prepared. It is "so far off" from that mystical Jerusalem where one day they will be found, put together, and collectively to constitute that Temple, which is still being built without hands nor the noise of metal tools. And this world, therefore, being but a transient, temporary one for us, is necessarily one of shadows, images, and merely "substituted secrets." It will be so until being raised not merely symbolically but in character and knowledge and consciousness to the sublime degree of Master Mason. We fit ourselves to learn something of the "genuine secrets," something of the living realities that lurk and live in concealment behind the outward show of things. All human life, having originated in the mystical "East" and journeyed into this world which, with us, is the "West," must return to its source. To quote again the verse of the Brother I have already cited;

> "From East to West the soul her journey takes;
> At many bitter founts, her fever slakes;
> Halts at strange taverns by the way to feast,
> Resumes her load, and painful progress makes
> Back to the East."

Using a series of dramatic representations, Masonry is intended to furnish those who care to discover its purport and take advantage of the hints it throws out in allegorical form, with examples and instructions by which our return to the "East" may be accelerated. It refers to no architecture of a mundane kind but to the architecture of the soul's life. It is not a religion, but a dramatized and intensified form of religious processes inculcated by every religious system.

Our teaching is purposely veiled in allegory and symbol, and its deeper significance does not appear on the surface of the ritual itself. This is partly in correspondence with human life itself and the world we live in, which are themselves but allegories and symbols of another life and the veils of another world, and partly intentional also so that only those who have respectful and understanding minds may receive the more hidden meaning of the doctrine of the Craft. The deeper secrets in Masonry, like the deeper secrets of life, are heavily veiled and closely hidden. They exist concealed beneath a great cloud, but no one knows anything about them. We also should know that they are "many and valuable" and are disclosed only to those who act upon the hint given in our lectures, "Seek and ye shall find; ask and ye shall have; knock and it shall be opened unto you." The search may be long and difficult, but great things cannot be acquired without effort. Still, it may be affirmed that to the candidate who is "properly prepared" (in a much fuller sense than we conventionally attach to that expression), there are doors leading from the Craft that, when knocked, will assuredly open and admit him to places and to the knowledge he lacks at present. For him who would enter upon the greater initiations, the same rule applies to that symbolically represented upon his first entrance into the Order. Still, it will no longer be a symbol but a realistic fact this time. He will find that a drawn sword is always threatening in front of him and that a cable tow is still around his neck. Danger awaits the candidate who would rush hastily and in a state of moral unfitness into the deeper mysteries of his being, which are indeed "serious, solemn, and awful." But, on the other hand, for him who has entered the path of Light, it is moral suicide to turn back.

And now, Brethren, to bring to an end this brief and imperfect survey of the deeper meaning and purposes of our Craft, I pray that what is now offered may help to prove to some of you a further restoration to that light which is, at all times, the predominant wish of our hearts. It rests with us whether Masonry remains for us what appears to be merely a series of symbolic rites on its outward and superficial side or whether we allow those symbols to pass into our lives and become realities therein. Whatever formalities we may have gone through in connection with our admission into the Order, we cannot believe to have been "regularly initiated" into Masonry so long as we regard the Craft as merely an incident of social life and treat its ceremonies as but rites of an archaic and superficial nature. The Craft, as I have already suggested, was given out to the world, from more secret sources still, as a grand experiment and means of grace and as an excellent opportunity for those who cared to avail themselves of what is little known and little taught outside certain sanctuaries of concealment. It was intended to furnish a synopsis, in dramatic form, of the spiritual regeneration of man and to throw out hints and suggestions that might lead those capable of discerning its deeper purpose and symbolism into still deeper initiations than the merely superficial ones enacted in our lodges. As on the external side of the Order, we may be called to occupy positions of honor and office in the Grand Lodge or may enter other Masonic grades outside the Craft. So also, upon its internal side, there are eminences to which we may be called that, while offering us no social distinction and no visible advancement, are yet really the true prizes, the most valuable attainments, of Masonic desire. To this goal, all may genuinely seek to do so and prepare the way for themselves by appropriating the truths beneath the superficial allegory and the symbolic veils of the Craft teaching. And since there seems today a genuine and widespread desire on the part of many members of the Order to enter into a fuller understanding of what the Order itself conceals rather than reveals, I feel I should not be discharging my duties as a Master in the Craft did I not take advantage of that position to share with them some measure at least of what I have been able to glean for myself.

And, finally, I must ask you to remember that, following the general design of our system, every Master of a Lodge is but a symbol and a substitution, and that behind him, behind all other grand officers of the Masonic hierarchy stands the Grand Master of all true Masons throughout the Universe, whether members of our Craft or not. To whom let us all bow in gratitude for the invaluable gift accorded to us in this our Order; and to whose protection, and to whose enlightening guidance into its deeper mysteries, I commend you all.

Footnotes
* *Strange Houses of Sleep* by A. E. Waite.

Chapter II.
Masonry as a Philosophy

IT is unclear if a higher Masonic consciousness is awakening in the Craft. Members of the Order are gradually becoming aware of the fact that much more than meets the eye and ear lies beneath the surface of Masonic doctrine and symbols. They are beginning to think for themselves instead of taking Freemasonry at face value or for granted. As their thoughts develop, previously unnoticed facts begin to assume prominence and significance. They perceive the Masonic system as something deeper than a code of elementary morality. They reflect that modern speculative Masonry perpetuates nothing more than the private associations that once existed in connection with the operative builders' trade. They recognize that there can be no peculiar virtue or interest in continuing to imitate the customs of ancient trade guilds for the mere sake of so doing or of keeping alive a costly organization for teaching men the elementary symbolism of a few building tools, supplemented by a considerable number of social pleasantries. Upon a bit of thought, it becomes evident that our Third Degree and the great central legend that forms the climax of the Craft system has no direct or practical bearing upon, or connection with, the trade of the Operative Mason. It may be urged that we have a great charity system and that the social side of our proceedings is a valuable and humanizing asset. Granted, other people and societies are as philanthropic and social, as we are. A secret society is not necessary to promote such ends. The discernment of such facts as these, then, suggests to us that the Craft has not yet entered into the full heritage of understanding its system and that side-matters connected with Masonry, which we have long emphasized so strongly, valuable in their own way as they are, are not the primary and proper work of the Order. The work of the Order is to initiate worthy candidates into certain secrets and mysteries. Suppose the Order fails to expound its secrets and mysteries and to confer actual initiations as distinguished from passing candidates through certain formal ceremonies. In that case, it is not fulfilling its original purpose, whatever other incidental good it may be doing.

Now, as these facts are the basis upon which this lecture proceeds, let me, at the outset, make my first point. As the progress in the Craft of every brother admitted into its ranks is by gradual, successive stages, the understanding of the Masonic system and doctrine is also a matter of gradual development. Stated in the simplest terms possible, the theory of Masonic progress is that every Member admitted to the Order enters a state of darkness and ignorance as to what Masonry teaches. Later on, he is supposed to be brought to light and knowledge. Putting it in other terms, he enters the Craft symbolically as a rough ashlar, and it is his duty to develop his character and understanding so that he may ultimately be a finished and perfect cube.

Now, the understanding of the Masonic scheme tends to develop along precisely similar lines. Its meaning is not discernible all at once. Unless our minds are properly prepared and our understandings carefully trained, we are unlikely to ever participate in the real secrets and mysteries of Masonry. However, we often watch the performance of external ceremonials or participate in them, depending on how proficient we may be in memorizing the rituals and instruction lectures. The first stage is the first conception of what Masonry involves. It is concerned merely with the surface value of the Craft doctrine. Beyond this stage most Masons never pass. This is the stage of knowledge in which the Craft is regarded as a social, semi-public, semi-secret community to which it is agreeable and advantageous to belong for sociable or even for ulterior purposes. This is the stage in which the goal of the Mason is to attain office, high preferment, and to wear a breast-full of decorations. It is one in which he takes a literal, superficial, and historical view of the subject-matter of the doctrine. He greatly values the ability to perform the ceremonial work with dignity and effectiveness and to know the instruction catechisms by heart so that no syllable is incorrectly rendered. It is deemed the height of Masonic proficiency, and after discharging these functions with a certain degree of credit, his idea is often to have the lodge closed as speedily as may be and get away to the repose of the festive board.

Now, all these things belong to what may be called the very rough-ashlar stage of the Masonic conception. I am not, of course, alluding to any individual Mason. I confess frankly to having come from within this category myself, and I think we may agree that we have all passed through the phase I have described because we knew nothing better and had no one to teach us something better. Let us not complain. Let's look at the Craft's progress during the last 150 years. We cannot but congratulate ourselves upon the enormous, if gradual, strides made in Masonic evolution and decorum, even in the rough-ashlar stage of our conception. Anyone familiar with the records of old Lodges will have been brought into close touch with times when almost every element of reverence and dignity seems to have been lacking. Lodges were held in the public rooms of taverns. Whatever official furniture decorated these primitive temples, quart-pots and "churchwardens" figured largely among the unauthorized equipment. In one of the great London galleries, a famous picture called "Night" hangs by the great artist and moralist of his age, Hogarth. His purpose was to depict a characteristic night scene in the streets of London as they appeared in his time. Among the typical specimens of depravity haunting those ill-lit streets, the great artist has held up to the scorn of all time the figure of a Freemason staggering home drunk, still wearing his apron and being assisted by the tyler of the lodge. No faithful Mason can regard this picture without a burning sense of shame and without registering a resolution to redeem the Craft from this stigma. We have, I hope, gone past such things as these. We have awakened to some sense of dignity and self-reverence. The Craft is well governed by its higher authorities, and individual lodges take pride in providing proper temples and conducting assemblies with due regard to the solemnity of Masonic doctrine. May the Order never relapse into the primitive and chaotic condition from which it has emerged.

But this improvement in matters of external reputation, great and welcome as it is, is not enough. To prevent the Order from settling down into a state of self-satisfaction with its social privileges and the agreeableness of friendly intercourse among its members, the improvement I have spoken of must be attended (and I believe it is destined to be attended) by an awakening to the deep significance of the Craft's internal purposes. And since I have referred to what I have termed the "rough-ashlar" concept of that purpose, you have the right to ask me now to state that loftier conception which may be regarded, in comparison, as the "perfect cube." I shall not attempt to state the answer to this inquiry in so many words. I invite you to consider this whole lecture to indicate the answer. To some extent, I endeavored to formulate that answer upon a previous occasion. Still, while I entered rather into the details and minutia of the Craft system and symbols, I shall treat the subject now upon broader lines and deal with Masonry in its wider and more philosophical aspect. I said on that occasion — and I must repeat it now — that in its broad and more central doctrine, Masonry was essentially a philosophical and religious system expressed in dramatic ceremonies. It is a system intended to supply answers to the three great questions that press so unavoidably upon the attention of every thoughtful man, and those are the subjects around which all religions and all philosophies move: What am I? Whence come I? Whither will go I? It is a truism to say that we all need a reliable answer to these questions in our quieter and more serious moments. Light upon them is "the predominant wish of our hearts," such light as we can obtain, whether from Masonry or elsewhere, depends on our philosophy of life and the rule of conduct that we regulate our life. In a larger sense, the Masonic candidate is presumed to have entered the Order in search of Light upon these problems, Light that he is presumed not to have succeeded in finding elsewhere. Suppose his candidature is actuated by any motive other than a genuine desire for knowledge upon *these* problems, which beyond all others are vital to his peace, and by a sincere wish to render himself serviceable to his fellow creatures by the help of that knowledge. In that case, his candidature is less than a worthy one. No man should be solicited to join the Order because, regarding these matters of sacred and meaningful import, the first springs of impulse *must* originate within the postulant himself. The first place of his preparation must always be in his heart, and it is to the crying and knocking of his inward need, and for no less a motive, that the door to the Mysteries is opened. The seeker enters in and finds help. At another stage of his symbolic progress, the candidate learns from his superior brethren that they, along with himself, are searching for something that is lost and which they have hopes of finding. Here, the great motive of this and all quests, as well as the clue to the real purpose of Masonry, appears prominently and is stated in emphatic terms. Masonry is the quest after something that has been lost. Now, what is it that could be lost? Consider the matter thus. Why should we, or the world at large, require systems of religion and philosophy? What is the motive and reason for the existence of a Masonic Order and the many other Orders of Initiation, both in the past and the present? Why should they exist at all? I might reduce the matter to the compass of a small and personal point by asking why are you reading this book and why I should have been striving for many years to acquire the information that enables me to give it? In his reflective moments, the answer is that every man realizes that some element of his being has become lost. He is conscious, if he is honest with himself, of the sense of moral imperfection, of ignorance, of a restricted knowledge about himself and his surroundings. He is aware, in short, of some radical deficiency in his constitution, which, were it but found and made good, would satisfy this craving for information, completeness, and perfection. It would "lead him from darkness to light" and put him beyond ignorance and the touch of the many ills that the flesh invites. The point is too obvious to need pressing further. The answer is to be found by referencing a great doctrine that forms the philosophical basis of all systems of religion and the great systems of the Mysteries and Initiation of antiquity, popularly known as the Fall of Man. How we may choose to regard this event—and throughout the history of the human race, it has been taught in innumerable ways and all manner of parables, allegories, myths, and legends—its sole and single meaning is that humanity as a whole has fallen away from its original parent-source and place. From being embedded in the eternal center of life, man has become projected to the circumference. In our present world, man is undergoing a period of restriction, ignorance, discipline, and experience that shall ultimately fit him to return to the center where he came and to which he properly belongs. "Paradise Lost" is the real theme of Masonry no less than of Milton, as it is also of all the ancient systems of the Mysteries. The Masonic doctrine emphasizes the fact and the sense of this loss. Beneath a veil of allegory describing the intention to build a certain temple that could not be finished because of an untimely disaster, Masonry implies that Humanity is the real temple whose building became obstructed. We are both the craftsmen and the building materials of what was intended to be an unparalleled structure. But owing to a certain unhappy event, we live here in this world where the genuine and full secrets of our nature are lost to us for the time being. We live where the limitations of physical life curtail the full powers of the soul of man and where, during our apprenticeship of probation and discipline, we have to put up with the substituted knowledge derivable through our limited and very fallible senses.

But, while Masonry emphasizes this great truth, it indicates also—and this is its great virtue and real purpose—the method by which we may regain that which is lost to us. It holds out the great promise that, with divine assistance and our industry, we currently possess genuine realities. Still, the imperfect shadows shall be restored to us, and patience and perseverance will eventually entitle every worthy man to participate in them. This subject is mirrored in miniature in the Craft ceremonial. The East of the Lodge is the symbolic center, the source of all light, the place of the throne of the Master of all life. The West, the place of the disappearing sun, is this world of imperfection and darkness from which the divine spiritual light is withdrawn and only shines by reflection. The ceremonies through which the candidate passes are symbolic of the stages of progress that every man—whether a formal member of the Craft or not. They can be viewed as a way of self-purification and self-building until he at length lies dead to his present natural self and is raised out of a state of imperfection and brought once more into perfect union with the Lord of life and glory into whose image he has thus become shaped and conformed.

In this greater sense, then, it is that Masonry may become for us—as indeed it was intended to become by those who instituted our present speculative system—a working philosophy for those brought within its influence. It supplies a need to those earnestly enquiring into the purpose and destiny of human life. It is a means of initiating into reliable knowledge those who feel that their understanding of life and their path of life have been but a series of irregular steps made at haphazard and under hoodwinked conditions as to the correctness of their steps. Not without good reason does our catechism assert that Masonry contains "many and invaluable secrets." But these, of course, are not the formal and symbolic signs, tokens, and words communicated ceremonially to candidates. Instead, they are secrets we instinctively keep locked up in our hearts' recesses and safe repositories. They are secrets of the deep and hidden things of the soul, about which we do not often talk. And, by instinct, we are not in the habit of communicating to any but such of our brethren and fellows who share with us a common and sympathetic interest in the deeper problems and mysteries of life.

Masonry is a modern perpetuation of great systems of initiation that have existed for the spiritual instruction of men in all parts of the world since the beginning of time. The reason for their existence has been apparent, resulting from the cardinal truth already alluded to, that man in his present natural state is inherently and radically imperfect. But, sooner or later, he becomes conscious of a sense of loss and deprivation and feels an imperative need to learn how to recover from that loss. The great world religions have been ordained to teach the same truths that the Mystery Systems have taught in their respective manners. Their teaching has always been twofold. An external, elementary, popular doctrine has always served the instruction of the masses, who are insufficiently prepared for deeper teaching. Concurrently, in addition to that, there has been an interior, advanced doctrine, a more secret knowledge, which has been reserved for riper minds and into which only proficient and properly prepared candidates who voluntarily sought to participate in it were initiated. Whether in ancient India, Egypt, Greece, Italy, or Mexico or among the Druids of Europe, temples of initiation have existed for those who felt the inward call to come apart from the multitude and to dedicate themselves to a long discipline of body and mind. They come with the view of acquiring the secret knowledge and developing the spiritual faculties using experimental initiation processes, of which our present ceremonies are the faint echo. It is far beyond my present scope to describe any of these great systems or the methods of initiation they employed.

But regarding them, I will ask you to accept my statement on two points: (1) although these great schools of the Mysteries have long dropped out of the public mind, they, or the doctrine they taught, have never ceased to exist; the hostility of official ecclesiasticism and the tendencies of a materialistic and commercial age have caused them to subside into extreme secrecy and concealment, but their initiates have never been absent from the world; and (2) that it was through the activity and foresight of some of these advanced initiates that our present system of speculative Masonry exists. You must not imply from this that modern Masonry is by any means a full or adequate presentation of these older and larger systems. It is but their pale and elementary shadow. But such as they are, and so far as they do go, our rituals and doctrine authentically embody a secret doctrine and a secret process that has always existed for the enlightenment of such aspirants. They have knocked at the door of certain secret sanctuaries in the confidence that that door would open and that they would find in due course that for which they were seeking. Those who instituted modern speculative Masonry some 250+ years ago took certain materials that spoke to their hearts. They took, that is, the elementary rites and symbols pertaining to medieval operative guilds of stone masons and transformed them into a system of religious-philosophic doctrine. Subsequently, from being related to the trade that deals in stones and bricks, Masonry retained certain analogies that the art of the practical stone-mason provided. It then became dedicated to wholly spiritual, religious, and philosophical purposes.

Perhaps the chief evidence of the transformation thus effected was incorporating the central legend and traditional history in our Third Degree. That legend can have had no relation to, or practical bearing upon, the operative builders' trade. I will ask you to reflect that no building of stone, temple, or other edifice capable of being built with hands has remained unfinished through the death of any professional architect such as Hiram Abiff. The principles of architecture, the genuine secrets of the building trade, are not and never have been lost. They are thoroughly well known, and the absurdity manifests in supposing that Masons of any kind are waiting for time or circumstances to restore any lost knowledge of how temporal buildings ought to be constructed. We know how to erect buildings today quite as well as our Hebrew forefathers who built the famous temple at Jerusalem, and indeed, a well-known architect has stated that most of our London churches are, both for size and ornamentation, far larger and more splendid than that temple ever was. Our duty then is to look behind the literal story, to pierce the veil of allegory contained in the great legend, and to grasp the significance of its true purport. That which is lost is to be found, we are told, with the Center. But suppose we enquire "What is a Center?" In that case, the average Mason will give you nothing more than the official, enigmatic, and not very luminous answer that it is a point within a circle from which every part of the circumference is equidistant. But what circle? And what circumference? There are no such things as centers or circles concerning ordinary buildings or architecture. And here, the average Mason is at an utter loss to explain. Press him further, "Why with the Center?" and again, he can only give you the elusive and perplexing answer, "Because that is a point from which a Master Mason cannot err," and you are no wiser.

Brethren, it is just this elusiveness, these intentional enigmas, this puzzle language, intended to put us on the scent of something deeper than the words themselves convey. If we fail to find, realize, and act upon the intention of what is veiled behind the letter of the rituals, we can scarcely claim to understand our doctrine. We can scarcely claim to have been regularly initiated, passed, and raised in the higher sense of those expressions, whatever ceremonies we have formally passed through. "The letter killeth, the spirit giveth life." Let us enquire about the spirit of this puzzle language.

The method of all great religious and initiatory systems has been to teach their doctrine in myth, legend, or allegory. As our first tracing-board lecture says, "The philosophers, unwilling to expose their mysteries to vulgar eyes, concealed their tenets and principles of philosophy under hieroglyphical figures," and our traditional history is one of these hieroglyphical figures. Now, the literally-minded never see behind the letter of the allegory. The initiated mind discerns the allegory's spiritual value. Part of the purpose of all initiation was, and still is, to educate the mind in penetrating the outward shell of all phenomena. The value of initiation depends upon how the inward truths are allowed to influence our thoughts and lives and awaken deeper powers of consciousness in us.

The legend of the Third Degree, in which the essence of Masonic doctrine exists, was brought into our system by advanced minds who derived their knowledge from other concealed sources. The legend is an adaptation of a very old one and lived in various forms long before its association with modern Masonry. In the guise of a story about the building of a temple by King Solomon in Jerusalem, they were promulgating the truth that I have alluded to before, and that is generally known as the Fall of Man. As our legend delivers, upon the literal side of it, a great king's purpose was erecting a superb structure. He was assisted in that work by another king who supplied the building materials, a skillful artificer whose business was to put these together according to a pre-ordained plan, and large companies of craftsmen and laborers. But in the course of the work, an evil conspiracy arose, resulting in the destruction of the chief artificer and preventing the completion of the building, which remains unfinished.

Now, I will ask you to observe that this legend cannot refer to any historical building built in the old vicinity of

Palestine. If we refer to the Bible as an authority, we will find that that temple was completed; it was afterward destroyed, rebuilt, and, again, on more than one occasion. Moreover, the biblical accounts do not refer to the conspiracy or the death of Hiram. On the other hand, they expressly state that Hiram "made an end of building" the temple and was completed in every way. It is clear then that we must keep the two subjects separate and recognize that the Masonic story deals with something quite distinct from the biblical story. What temple then is referred to? The temple, brethren, that is still incomplete and unfinished is none that can be built with hands. It is that temple of which all material edifices are but the types and symbols: it is the temple of the collective body of humanity itself. The great initiate St. Paul said, "Know ye not that ye are the temple of God?" A perfect humanity was the great Temple, which, in the counsels of the Most High, was intended to be reared in the mystical Holy City, of which the local Jerusalem was the type. The three great Master-builders, Solomon and the two Hirams are a triad corresponding after a manner with the Holy Trinity of the Christian religion; Hiram Abiff being the chief architect, he "by whom all things were made" and "in whom (as St. Paul said, using Masonic language) the whole building fitly framed together groweth unto a holy temple in the Lord." The material of this mystical temple was the souls of men, at once the living stones, the fellow craftsmen, and collaborators with the divine purpose.

However, during this ideal temple's construction, something wrecked the scheme and delayed its fulfillment indefinitely. This was the Fall of Man, the conspiracy of the craftsmen. Turn to the book of Genesis; you will find the same subject related to the allegory of Adam and Eve. As you know, they were intended for perfection and happiness, but their Creator's project became nullified by disobedience to certain conditions. I will ask you to observe that our Masonic conspirators committed their offense precisely. They had been forbidden to eat of the Tree of Knowledge, or, in Masonic language, they were under obligation "not to attempt to extort the secrets of a superior degree" which they had not attained. The Hebrew word Hiram means *Guru*, teacher of "supreme knowledge," divine light and wisdom, and the liberty that comes in addition. But this knowledge is only for the perfected man. It is that knowledge that Hiram said was "known to but three in the world," *i.e.*, known only in the counsels of the Divine Trinity, but it is the knowledge that with patience and perseverance, every Mason, every child of the Creator, "may in due time become entitled to a participation in." But just as Adam and Eve's attempt to obtain illicit knowledge caused their expulsion from Eden and defeated the divine purpose until they and their posterity should regain the Paradise they had lost, so also the completion of the great mystical Temple was prevented for the time being by the conspirators' attempt to extort from Hiram the Master's secrets. Its construction is delayed until time and circumstances—God's time, and the circumstances we create for ourselves—restore to us the lost and genuine secrets of our nature and the divine purpose in us.

The tragedy of Hiram Abiff is not the record of a brutal murder. It is a parable of universal loss, an allegory of the breakdown of a divine scheme. We are dealing with no calamity that occurred during the erection of a building but with a moral disaster to universal humanity. Hiram is slain; in other words, the faculty of enlightened wisdom has been cut off from us. Owing to that disaster, humanity is today in this world of imperfect knowledge, limited faculties, checkered happiness, perpetual toil, death, and frequent bitterness and pain; our life here is (to use a poet's words):

> "An ever-moaning battle in the mist,
> Death in all life and lying in all love;
> The meanest having power upon the highest,
> And the high purpose broken by the worm."

The temple of human nature is unfinished, and we need to know how to complete it. The desire for plans and designs to regulate individual and social life disorders indicates that some heavy calamity has befallen us. The absence of a clear and guiding principle in the world's life reminds us of the utter confusion into which the absence of that Supreme Wisdom, which is personified as Hiram, has thrown us all and causes every reflective mind to attribute to some fatal catastrophe his mysterious disappearance. We all long for that light and wisdom lost to us. Like the craftsmen searching for the body, we go different ways to find what is lost. Many of us do not discover importance throughout our lives. We seek it in pleasure, in work, in all the varied occupations and diversions of our lives. We seek it in intellectual pursuits, in religion, in Masonry. Those who search farthest and deepest are those who become most conscious of the loss and who are compelled to cry, "Machabone! Macbenah! The Master is smitten," or, as the Christian Scriptures word it, "They have taken away my Lord, and I know not where they have laid him."

Hiram Abiff is slain. The great light and wisdom ordained to guide and enlighten humanity is taken from us. The full blaze of light and perfect knowledge to be ours has vanished, but in the Divine Providence, there remains a glimmering light in the East. In a dark world, from which, as it were, the sun has disappeared, we still have our five senses and our rational faculties to work with, and these provide us with the substituted secrets that must distinguish us before we regain the genuine ones.

Where is Hiram buried? We are taught that the Wisdom of the Most High — personified as King Solomon — ordered him to be interred in a fitting tomb outside the Holy City. It was to be "in a grave from the center 3 feet between N. and S., 3 feet between E. and W., and 5 feet or more perpendicular." Where, Brethren, do you imagine that grave to be? Can you locate it by following these minute details of its situation? You probably have never thought of the matter as something other than an ordinary burial outside the walls of a geographical Jerusalem. But the grave of Hiram is us. Each of us is the tomb in which the smitten Master is interred. It is a further sign of our benightedness if we don't know it. At the center of ourselves, deeper than any dissecting knife can reach or than any physical investigation can fathom, lies buried the "vital and immortal principle." The "glimmering ray" that affiliates us to the Divine Center of all life and that is never wholly extinguished, however evil or imperfect our lives may be. We are the grave of the Master. The lost guiding light is buried at the center of ourselves. High as your hand may reach upwards or downwards from the center of your own body—*i.e.*, 3 feet between N. and S. far as it can reach to right or left of the middle of your person—*i.e.*, 3 feet between W. and E.—and 5 feet or more perpendicular—the height of the human body—these are the indications by which our cryptic ritual describes the tomb of Hiram Abiff at the center of ourselves. He is buried "outside the Holy City," in the same sense that the posterity of Adam has all been placed outside the walls of Paradise, for "nothing unclean can enter into the holy place," which elsewhere in our Scriptures is called the Kingdom of Heaven.

What, then, is this "Center"? By reviving and using it, may we hope to regain the secrets of our lost nature? As the Divine Life and Will is the center of the universe and controls it, as the sun is the center and life-giver of our solar system, a vital, immortal principle exists at the secret center of individual human life, the spirit, and the spiritual will of man. This is the faculty, by using which (when we have found it) we can never stumble. It is a point within the circle of our nature and, living as we do in this physical world, the circle of our existence is bounded by two grand parallel lines; "one representing Moses; the other King Solomon," that is to say, law and wisdom; the divine ordinances regulating the universe on the one hand; the divine "wisdom and mercy that follow us all the days of our life" on the other. It is true that the Mason who keeps himself circumscribed cannot stumble.

Masonry, then, is a system of religious philosophy that provides us with a doctrine of the universe and our place in it. It indicates whence we come and whither we may return. It has two purposes. Its first purpose is to show that man has fallen from a high and holy center to the circumference or externalized condition we live in. This indicates that those who so desire may regain that center by finding the center in themselves. Since Deity is as a circle whose center is everywhere, it follows that a Divine Center, a "vital and immortal principle," exists within ourselves by developing which we may hope to regain our lost and primal stature. The Craft doctrine's second purpose is to define how the center may be found within ourselves. This teaching is embodied in the discipline and ordeals delineated in the three degrees. The Masonic doctrine of the Center — or, in other words, the Christian axiom that "the Kingdom of Heaven is within you" — is nowhere better stated than by the poet Browning:

> "Truth is within ourselves. It takes no rise
> From outward things, whate'er you may believe.
> There is an inmost centre in ourselves
> Where truth abides in fullness, and to know
> Rather consists of finding a way
> Whence the imprisoned splendour may escape
> Then, by effecting entrance for a light
> Supposed to be without."

Brethren, may we all come to the knowledge of how to "open the lodge upon the center" of ourselves and so realize in our own conscious experience the finding of the "imprisoned splendor" hidden in the depths of our being, whose rising within ourselves will bring us peace and salvation. How, then, does the Craft doctrine prescribe for the liberation of this imprisoned center? Its first injunctions are those of our first degree. There must be purity of thought and purpose. I need scarcely remind you that the word candidate derives from the Latin *candidus*, white (in the sense of purity), or that our postulants, before entering the lodge, leave behind them in the precincts the garments that belong to the fashion of the outer world whose ideals they are desirous of relinquishing. They enter the Lodge clad in white, emblematic of the blamelessness of their thought and the purification of their lives. As this symbolic white clothing is worn during each of the three degrees, it is as though the seeker, after the High Light of the Center, must always come uttering the triple ascription, "Holy, Holy, Holy," as the token of the threefold purity of body, soul, and spirit, which is essential to the achievement of his quest. He has left all money and metals behind him, for the gross things of this world are superfluous in the world that resides within. If any waste of thought or character imperfections remain in him, he will find it impossible to attain the consciousness of his highest self. He will learn that he must renounce them and begin again and that his attempt at real initiation must be repeated.

A spirit of universal sympathy must animate him. Financial doles and practical relief to the impoverished and distressed are admirable practices. Still, they do not exhaust the meaning of charity as Masonry intends. Paying a few coins to philanthropic institutions is scarcely a fulfillment of St. Paul's definition of charity so often read in our lodges.

There is a far larger sense of brotherhood than the limited conventional one obtained among members of a common association. There is that deep sense in which a man feels himself not only in fraternity with his fellow men, whether Masonically his brethren or not, but realizes himself as a brother to all. That is part of the universal life that thrills through all things.

Passing from these primary qualifications, we proceed to what is signified by our second degree, wherein inculcated the analysis and cultivation of the mental and rational faculties, the study of the secrets of man's marvelous, complex, psychical nature. The relation of these with the still higher and spiritual part of him which, in turn, he may learn to trace "even to the throne of God Himself," with which he is affiliated at the root essence of his being. These studies, so lightly touched upon in our passing ceremony, so glibly referred to as we recite our ritual when undertaken with the seriousness that is attached to them in the old mystery systems, are not without just reason described in our own words as "serious, solemn and awful." The depths of human nature and self-knowledge, the hidden mysteries of the soul of man, are not probed into with impunity except by the "properly prepared." The man who does so has, as it were, a cable tow around his neck because he *must* continue seeking once stirred by a genuine desire for the higher knowledge that real initiation is intended to confer. He can never turn back on what he learns thereof without committing moral suicide. He can never again be the same man he was before he gained a glimpse of those hidden mysteries of life. And as the Angel stood with a flaming sword at the entrance of Eden to guard the way to the Tree of Life, so will the man whose initiation is not a conventional one finds himself threatened at the door of the higher knowledge by opposing invisible forces if he rashly rushes forward in a state of moral unfitness into the deep secrets of the Center. It is better to remain ignorant than embark upon this unknown sea unwisely and without being prepared and possessing the proper passports.

Eventually, the aspirant learns the great truth embodied in the third degree: that he who would be raised to perfection and regain what he has long realized has been lost to himself may do so only by utter self-rejection. By a symbolic dying to the uninitiated outer world. The third degree, brethren, is an exposition in the dramatic ceremonial of the text: "Whoso would save his life must lose it." Beneath the allegory of the death of the Master — and remember that it *is* an allegory — is expressed the universal truth that mystical death must precede mystical rebirth. "Know ye not that ye must be born again?" "Unless a grain of corn falls to the ground and die, it abideth alone; if it dies, it bringeth forth much fruit." And it is only thus that all Master Masons can be raised from a figurative (not a physical) death to a regenerated state and the full stature of human nature.

The path of proper initiation into the fullness of life through a symbolic death to one's lower self is the path called in the Scriptures *the narrow way*, of which it is also said that few find it. It is the narrow path between the Pillars, for Boaz and Jachin stand impliedly at the entrance of every Masonic Temple. Between them, we pass each time we enter the lodge. Very great prominence is accorded these pillars in the ritual, but very little explanation of their importance is given. It is necessary to know something of their great significance. To deal with them fully would require an entire lecture on this one subject, and even then, there would have to remain unsaid regarding these great symbols, which is unsuited to treatment in a general lecture.

The pillars form and have always formed, a prominent feature in the temples of all great systems of religion and initiation, whether Masonic or not. They have been incorporated into Christian architecture. If you recall the construction of York Minster or Westminster Abbey, you will recognize the pillars in the two great towers flanking the main entrance to those cathedrals at the west end of the structure. Non-Masons, therefore, enter these temples, as we do, between the pillars in the West. They look through the pillars along the straight path that leads to the high altar, just as the Mason's symbolic passage is also from the West to the throne in the East. That path is, as it were, the straight path of life, beginning in this outer world and terminating at the throne, or altar, in the

East. Many centuries before our Bible was written or the temple of Solomon described in the Books of Kings and Chronicles was thought of; the two pillars were used in the great temples of the Mysteries in Egypt. A great annual public festival was the setting up of the pillars. What, then, did they signify?

I can deal with the subject, but it is very superficial here. In one of their accounts, they stand for what is known in Eastern philosophy as the "pairs of opposites." Everything in nature is dual and can only be known in contrast with its opposite. At the same time, the two, in combination, produce a metaphysical third: their synthesis and perfect balance. Thus, we have good and evil, light and darkness (and one of the pillars was always white and the other black), active and passive, positive and negative, yes and no, outside and inside, man and woman. Neither of these is complete without the other; they form stability. Morning and evening unite to form the full day. Man is proverbially imperfect without his "better half," woman. The two marry to impart strength to each other and to establish their common house. Physical science shows that all matter is composed of positive and negative electric forces in perfect balance. Things would disintegrate and disappear if they did not stand firm in perfect union. Every drop of healthy blood in our bodies combines red and white corpuscles. The balance establishes strength and health, while disease follows a lack of balance. The pillars, therefore, typify, in one of their aspects, the perfect integrity of body and soul, which are essential to achieving spiritual perfection. In ancient philosophy, all things created are composed of fire and water. Fire is their spiritual element, and water is their material element. So, the pillars also represented these universal properties. In one of the Apocryphal Scriptures (2 Esdras, 7; 7-8), the path to true wisdom and life is spoken of as an entrance between a fire on the right hand and a deep water on the left, and so narrow and painful that only one man may go through it at once. This alludes to the narrow and painful path of real initiation, of which our entrance into the lodge between the pillars is a symbol.

Now, all great symbols are shadowed forth in the person of man himself. The human organism is the true lodge that must be opened. Wherein the great Mysteries are to be found, and our lodge rooms are so built and furnished as to typify the human organism. The lower and physical part of us is animal and earthy. It rests, like the base of Jacob's ladder, upon the earth. While our higher portion is spiritual and reaches the heavens. These two portions of us are in perpetual conflict. The spiritual and the sensual are ever warring against one another. He is the wise man who has learned to affect a perfect balance between them. He has learned to strengthen himself so that his inward house stands firm against all weakness and temptation. In another sense, the two pillars may be seen as exemplified in the human body. There are our two legs, upon which we must stand firm to acquire a perfect physical balance. And having discovered this simple truth and seeing that the path of true initiation (spiritual rebirth) is an arduous and painful progress for him who undertakes it. Let me ask you to consider a great mystery that we perhaps rarely think of because of its frequency and our familiarity with it. I refer to the incident—the great mystery—of childbirth. Brethren, every child born into this world comes into this life as if into a great house of initiation. We pass through pain, joy, good and bad, ignorance and wisdom. The act of physical birth is an image and a foreshadowing of that mystical rebirth and of that passing through a straight gate and a narrow way in a deeper sense. Without which it is written that a man shall not enter into the Kingdom of Heaven.

The regenerated man has passed through the phases of the Masonic degrees not merely in ceremonial form but in essential experience. He alone is worthy of the title of Master Mason in the building of the Temple, which is not made with hands but is being built invisibly out of the souls of just men made perfect. Not only is this temple being built in this world, but only the foundations of the intended structure are perceptible here. The Craft contemplates other and loftier planes of life, different stories of the vast structure than this in which we live and work. Just as our Craft organization has its higher assemblies and councils in the form of the Grand Lodges and other bodies that regulate and minister to the needs of the craft lodges, so in the mighty system of the universal structure, there are grades of higher life, hierarchies of celestial beings working and ministering in the loftier portions of the building, beyond our present sight. And here, at the head of our limited and temporal brotherhood, there rules a Grand Master. Over the cosmic system presides the Great Architect and Most Worshipful, Grand Master of all, whose officers are Holy Angels. The recognition of this truth may tend to consecrate us in the discharge of the little symbolic part we severally perform in the system, which is the image of the great scheme.

The world at large, Brethren, is as it were, but one great lodge and place of initiation, of which our Masonic Lodges are the little mirrors. Mother Earth is also the Mother Lodge of us all. As its vast work goes on, souls descend into it and are being called out of it at the knocks of some great unseen Warden of life and death. This Warden calls them here to labor and summons them hence for refreshment. Thus, although our after-proceedings have no formal place in the Masonic system, they still play a striking and appropriate part calculated to awaken us to the deep significance of our customary conviviality. On such occasions, we drink the toast of "the King and the Craft," remembering our heavenly sovereign and Masonic comrades worldwide as loyal subjects and loving brethren. But here again, I would ask every Master who gives and every brother who drinks this toast to lift his thoughts to a greater King and a larger craft than our limited and symbolic fraternity. I would remind you how in the Christian Mysteries there was another Master whom unconsciously we imitate, who also after supper took the cup and, when he had given thanks to the King of kings, pledged himself, as it were, to that larger Craft which is co-extensive with humanity itself. In so, directing them in this manner to show forth symbolically a certain great mystery until his coming again. But this, Brethren, is none other than what is implied in our Masonic words when we are also directed to use certain substituted secrets until time and circumstances shall restore the genuine ones to us.

In submitting these thoughts to you, it may be claimed that Masonry offers to those capable of appreciating it a working philosophy and a practical rule of life. It discloses to us the scheme of the universe—a scheme once shattered and arrested but left in the hands of humanity to restore. It indicates our place, purpose, and destiny in that universe. It is a great house of instruction and initiation into the Mysteries of a larger and fuller life than the unenlightened world, which is yet ripe for appreciation. Let us, therefore, value and endeavor fully to appreciate its mysteries. Let us also be careful not to cheapen the Order by failing to realize its meaning and by admitting to its ranks those who are unready or unfit to understand its importance. At the outset of this lecture, I said that some Masons are beginning to awaken to a larger consciousness of the true meaning and purpose of our Craft. I speak now at the end, Brethren! Lift your hearts; open the shutters of your minds and imaginations. Learn to see in Masonry something more than a parochial system enjoining elementary morality, performing perfunctory rites that are little more than meaningless. Our Order was never meant to be merely an agreeable accessory to social life. But look at what we are: a living philosophy, a vital guide upon those matters that are the most sacred and urgent to our ultimate well-being. Realize that its secrets, which are "many and invaluable," are not upon the surface. They are not those of the tongue but of the heart, and its mysteries are those eternal ones that speak to the spirit rather than to the body of man. And with this knowledge, dress yourselves and enter the lodge—not merely the lodge room of our symbolic Craft but the larger lodge of life. It is here where, silently and without the sound of a metal tool, the perpetual work of rebuilding the unfinished and invisible temple of which the mystical stones and timber are the souls of men is proceeding. In that rebuilding, men and women who, while formally not members of our Craft, are still unconsciously Masons in the best of senses are taking part. For whosoever is carefully and deliberately "squaring his stone" is fitting themselves for their place in the "intended structure," which one day will become manifest to our clearer vision and will appear "more like the work of the Great Architect of the Universe than that of human hands." Upon us Masons rests the responsibility attaching to our privilege, and it must be our aim to enter into the full heritage of understanding and practicing the system to which we belong.

CHAPTER III.
Further Notes on Craft Symbolism

"There is no darkness but ignorance." (*Shakespeare*). "Lighten our darkness, we beseech Thee, and defend us from all perils and dangers of this night." (*Anglican Liturgy*).

"Belov'd All-Father, and all you gods that haunt this place, grant me to be beautiful in the inner man, and all I have of outer things to be one with those within! May I count only the wise man rich, and may my store of gold be such as none but the good can bear. Anything more? That prayer, I think, is enough for me!" (*Prayer of Socrates*).

IN the Lecture on the First Degree tracing board, Masonry is "an art founded on the principles of Geometry" and "a science dealing with the cultivation and improvement of the human mind." Its usages and customs are also said to have derived "from the ancient Egyptians whose philosophers, unwilling to expose their mysteries to vulgar eyes, conceal their principles and philosophy under signs and symbols," still perpetuated in the Masonic Order.

The Instruction Lectures associated with each degree of the Craft purport to expound the system's doctrine and interpret the symbols and rituals. However, these lectures themselves have a similar need for interpretation. Indeed, they are contrived with very great cunning and concealment. Their compilers were confronted with the dual task of giving a faithful, if partial, expression of esoteric doctrine and, at the same time, masking it so that its complete sense would not be understood without some effort or enlightenment. For the uninitiated, what was offered would convey little or nothing to those unworthy of, or unripe for, the "gnosis" or wisdom-teaching. They successfully discharged that task in a way that provokes admiration from those who can appreciate it for their profound knowledge of, and insight into, the science of self-knowledge and regeneration. They were Initiates of an advanced type, well versed in the secret tradition and philosophy of the Mystery systems of the past and acutely perceptive of the deeper and mystical sense of the Holy Scriptures to which they constantly make luminous reference.

It is not possible to discuss these explanatory lectures in complete detail. However, we will proceed to discuss some of their more prominent topics and elaborate on the subject matter of our previous papers.

Attention must first be called to "Geometry," the art upon which the entire system is founded. To the ordinary man, Geometry means nothing more than the branch of mathematics associated with Euclid's problems, a subject unrelated to Masonic ceremonies and ideals. Therefore, another explanation of the term must be sought.

Geometry was one of the "seven noble arts and sciences" of ancient philosophy. It means the science of earth measurement. But the "earth" of the ancients did not mean, as it does to us, this physical planet. It meant the primordial substance, or undifferentiated soul-stuff from which we human beings have been created, the "mother earth" from which we have all sprung and to which we must all undoubtedly return. Man was made, the Scriptures teach, out of the dust of the ground, and it is that ground, that earth or fundamental substance of his being, which requires to be "measured" in the sense of investigating and understanding its nature and properties. No competent builder erects a structure without first satisfying himself with the nature of the materials he proposes to build. In the speculative, or spiritual, "royal art" of Masonry, no Mason can properly build the temple of his soul without first understanding the nature of the raw material he has to work with and upon.

Geometry, therefore, is synonymous with self-knowledge, the understanding of the basic substance of our being, its properties, and potentialities. Over the ancient temples of initiation was inscribed the sentence "Know thyself and thou shalt know the universe and God," a phrase which implies in the first place that the uninitiated man is without knowledge of himself, and in the second place that when he attains that knowledge he will realize himself to be no longer the separate distinctive individual he now supposes himself to be, but to be a microcosm or summary of all that is and to be identified with the Being of God.

Masonry is the science of attaining that supreme knowledge and is, therefore, rightly said to be founded on the principles of Geometry as thus defined.

But do not let it be supposed that the physical matter of which our mortal bodies are composed is the "earth." Our bodies are corruptible transitory stuff that merely forms a temporary encasement of our souls' imperishable true "earth." Our bodies are that substance that enables them to enter sense-relations with the physical world. The distinction must be grasped and held in mind, for Masonry must deal not so much with the transient outward body as with the eternal inward being of man. However, the outward body is temporarily involved with the latter. Man's immortal soul is a ruined temple and needs to be rebuilt upon the principles of spiritual science. The mortal body of it, with its unruly wills and affections, stands in the way of that achievement. The rubble must be cleared before the new foundations can be set and the new structure reared. Yet even rubble can be made to serve practical purposes when rearranged and worked into a new building. Accordingly, man's outer temporal nature can be disciplined and utilized to reconstruct himself. However, to affect this reconstruction, he must first thoroughly understand the material he has to work with and upon. For this purpose, he must be acquainted with "the form of the lodge."

The Form of the Lodge

This is officially described as "an oblong square; in length between East and West, in breadth between North and South, in depth from the surface of the earth to its center, and even as high as the heavens."

This is interpretable as alluding to the human individual. Man himself is a lodge. And just as the Masonic lodge is "an assemblage of brethren and fellows met to expatiate upon the mysteries of the Craft," so individual man is a composite being made up of various properties and faculties assembled in him with a view to their harmonious interaction and working out the purpose of life. It must always be remembered that everything in Masonry is symbolic of *man* and his human constitution and spiritual evolution. Accordingly, the Masonic lodge is sacramental to the individual Mason as he is when he seeks admission to a lodge. A man's first entry into a lodge symbolizes his first entry into the science of knowing himself.

A four-square or four-sided building symbolizes his organism. This is per the ancient philosophical doctrine that four is the arithmetical symbol of everything that has manifested or physical form. Spirit, which is unmanifest and not physical, is expressed by the number three and the triangle. But Spirit, which has so far projected itself to become objective and wear a material form or body, is denoted by the number four and the quadrangle or square. Hence, the Hebrew name of Deity, known and worshipped in this outer world, was the great unspeakable name of four letters or Tetragrammaton, while the cardinal points of space are also four. Every manifested thing is a compound of the four essential metaphysical elements called by the ancients: fire, water, air, and earth. Therefore, the lodge's four-sidedness is also a reminder that the human organism is compounded of those four elements in balanced proportions. "Water" represents the psychic nature; "Air," the mentality; "Fire," the will and nervous force; while "Earth" is the condensation in which the other three become stabilized and encased.

But it is a duplicated square because man's organism does not consist of his physical body alone. The physical body has its "double" or ethereal counterpart in the astral body, an extension of the physical nature and a compound of the same four elements in an impalpable and more tenuous form. Therefore, the oblong spatial form of the lodge must be considered referable to the physical and ethereal nature of man in the conjunction in which they consist in each of us.

The four sides of the lodge are of further significance. The East of the lodge represents man's spirituality, his highest and most spiritual mode of consciousness. For most, spirituality is still latent and slumbering. It becomes active only in moments of stress or deep emotion. The West (or polar opposite of the East) represents his usual rational understanding, the consciousness he employs in temporal everyday affairs, his material-mindedness, or, as we might say, his "common sense." Midway between these East and West extremes is the South, the halfway house and meeting place of the spiritual intuition and the rational understanding; the point denoting abstract intellectuality and our intellectual power develops to its highest, just as the sun attains its meridian splendor in the South. The antipodes of this is the North, the sphere of benightedness and ignorance, referable to merely sense reactions and impressions received by that lowest and least reliable mode of perception, our physical sense-nature.

Thus, the four sides of the Lodge point to four different yet progressive modes of consciousness available to us. Sense impression (North), reason (West), intellectual ideation (South), and spiritual intuition (East) make up our four possible ways of knowledge. Of these, the ordinary man employs only the first two or perhaps three following his development and education, and his outlook on life and understanding of truth are correspondingly restricted and imperfect. Full and perfect knowledge is possible only when the deep-seeing vision and consciousness of man's spiritual principle have been awakened and repeatedly added to his other cognitive faculties. This is possible only to the true Master, who has all four methods of knowledge at his disposal in perfect balance and adjusted like the four sides of the lodge. Hence, the place of the Master and Past Masters is always in the East.

The "depth" of the lodge ("from the surface of the earth to its center") refers to the distance or difference of degree between the hollow consciousness of our earthly mentality and the supreme divine degree of consciousness resident at man's spiritual center when he has become able to open his lodge upon that center and to function in and with it.

The "height" of the lodge ("even as high as the heavens") implies that the range of consciousness possible to us when we have developed our potentialities to the fullest. Man, who has sprung from the earth and developed through the lower kingdoms of nature to his present rational state, has yet to complete his evolution by becoming a god-like being and unifying his consciousness with the Omniscient—to promote what is and always has been the sole aim and purpose of all Initiation.

To attain this expansion of consciousness, to scale this "height," is achieved "by the use of a ladder of many rounds or staves, but of three principal ones, Faith, Hope and Charity," of which the greatest and most productive is the last. That is to say, there are innumerable ways of developing one's consciousness to higher degrees, and every common-place daily experience may contribute to that end if it is rightly interpreted. Its purpose in the general pattern of our life scheme can be discerned. Yet even these should be subordinate to the three chief qualifications, namely, Faith in the possibility of attaining the end in view; Hope, or a persistent, earnest desire for its fulfillment; and finally, an unbounded Love which, seeking God in all men and all things, gradually identifies the mind and nature of the aspirant with that ultimate Good upon which his thought, desire, and gaze should be persistently directed.

It is important to note here that this enlargement of consciousness is not dependent upon intellectual attainments, learning, or book knowledge. These may be, and indeed are, lesser rungs of the ladder of attainment, but they are not numbered among the principal ones. Compare St. Paul's words, "Though I have all knowledge and have not love, I am nothing," and those of a medieval mystic, "By love, He may be gotten and holden, but by wit and understanding never."

The lodge is "supported by three grand pillars, Wisdom, Strength and Beauty." Again, the references are not to the external meeting place but to a triplicity of properties resident in the individual soul, which will become increasingly manifest in the aspirant as he progresses and adapts himself to the Masonic discipline. As is written of the youthful Christian Master, "he increased in wisdom and stature and in favor with God and man," so will it also become true of the neophyte Mason who aspires to Mastership. He will become conscious of an increase of perceptive faculty and understanding. He will become aware of having tapped a previously unsuspected source of power, giving him enhanced mental strength and self-confidence. There will become observable in the neophyte developing graces of character, speech, and conduct that were previously foreign to him.

The Floor, or groundwork of the lodge, a checker-work of black and white squares, denotes the dual quality of everything connected with terrestrial life and the physical groundwork of human nature—the mortal body and its appetites and affections. "The web of our life is a mingled yarn, good and ill together," wrote Shakespeare. Everything material is characterized by inextricably interblended good and evil, light and shade, joy and sorrow, positive and negative. What is good for me may be evil for you; pleasure is generated from pain and ultimately degenerates into pain again. What is right to do at one moment may be wrong in the next. I am intellectually exalted today and then tomorrow, I am correspondingly depressed and benighted. The dualism of these opposites governs us in everything. Experience of it is prescribed for us until having learned and outgrown its lesson, we are ready for advancement to a condition where we outgrow the sense of this checker-work existence, and those opposites cease to be perceived as opposites. Still, they are realized as a unity or synthesis. To find unity or synthesis is to know the peace that passes understanding — *i.e.*, which surpasses our present experience because the darkness and the light are alike in it. Our present concepts of good and evil, joy and pain, are transcended and found sublimated in a condition combining both. This lofty condition is represented by the indented border skirting the black and white checker-work, even as the Divine Presence and Providence surround and embrace our temporal organisms in which those opposites are inherent.

Why is the checker floor-work given such prominence in the lodge furniture? The answer is to be found in the statement in the Third Degree Ritual: "The square pavement is for the High Priest to walk upon." Now, it is not merely the Jewish High Priest of centuries ago that is referred to here, but the individual member of the Craft, for every Mason, is intended to be the High Priest of his temple and to make of it a place where he and Deity may meet. Being in this dualistic world, every living being, whether a Mason or not, walks upon the square pavement of mingled good and evil in every action of his life so that the floor cloth symbolizes an elementary philosophical truth common to us all. But, for us, the words "walk upon" imply much more than that. They mean that he who aspires to be master of his fate and captain of his soul must walk upon these opposites in the sense of transcending and dominating them, trampling upon his lower sensual nature, and keeping it beneath his feet in subjection and control. He must rise above the motley of good and evil, to be superior and indifferent to the ups and downs of fortune, the attractions and fears governing ordinary men and swaying their thoughts and actions this way or that. His object is the development of his innate spiritual potencies, and it is impossible that these should develop so long as he is overruled by his material tendencies and the fluctuating emotions of pleasure and pain that they give birth to. By rising superior to these and attaining serenity and mental equilibrium under any circumstances, the enlightened Mason truly "walks upon" the checkered groundwork of existence and the conflicting tendencies of his more material nature.

The lodge's Covering is shown in sharp contrast to its black-and-white flooring and is described as "a celestial canopy of divers colors, even the heavens."

If the flooring symbolizes man's earthy, sensual nature, the ceiling typifies his ethereal nature, his "heavens," and the properties resident therein. The one is the reverse and the opposite pole of the other. His material body is visible and densely composed. His ethereal surround, or "aura," is tenuous and invisible (save to clairvoyant vision) and like the fragrance shared by a flower. Its existence will be doubted by those unprepared to accept what is not physically verifiable. Still, the Masonic student, who will be called upon to accept many such truths provisionally until he knows them as certainties, should reflect (1) that he has entered the Craft with the professed object of receiving light upon the nature of his being, (2) that the Order engages to assist him to that light regarding matters of which he is admittedly ignorant, and that its teachings and symbols were devised by wise and competent instructors in such matters, and (3) that a humble, docile and receptive mental attitude towards those symbols and their meanings will better conduce to his advancement than a critical or hostile one.

The fact that man throws off, or radiates from himself, an ethereal surround or "covering" is testified to by the haloes shown in works of art about the persons of saintly character. The unsaintly are not so distinctive, not because they are not so surrounded, but because in their case, the "aura" exists as but an irregularly shaped and colored cloud reflecting their typical undisciplined mentality and passional nature, as the rain clouds reflect the sunlight in different tints. The "aura" of the man, with his mentality clean and his passions and emotions well in hand, becomes a correspondingly orderly and shapely encasement of clearly defined form and iridescence, regularly striated like the colors of the spectrum or the rainbow. Biblically, this "aura" is described as a "coat of many colors" and as having characterized Joseph, the greatest of the sons of Jacob, in contrast with that patriarch's less morally and spiritually developed sons who were not lauded by any such coat.

In Masonry, the equivalent of the halo is the symbolic clothing worn by Provincial and Grand Lodge Officers. This is of deep blue, heavily fringed with gold, in correspondence with the deep blue center and luminous circumference of flame. "His ministers are flames of fire." Provincial and Grand Lodge Officers are drawn from Past Masters in the Craft, from those who theoretically have attained sanctity, regeneration, and Mastership of themselves and have joined the Grand Lodge above, where they "shine as the stars."

It follows from all this that the Mason who seriously yields himself to the discipline of the Order is not merely improving his character and chastening his thoughts and desires. At the same time, he unconsciously builds up an inner ethereal body that will form his clothing or covering when his transitory outer body passes away. "There are celestial bodies and bodies terrestrial [. . .] and as we *have* borne the image of the earthly, we also *shall* bear the image of the heavenly." And the celestial body must be built up out of the rerouted properties of the terrestrial one. This is one of the secrets and mysteries of the progression of regeneration and self-transmutation, the promotion of which the Craft was designed. This is the true temple building of which Masonry is concerned. The Apron, the Masonic symbol of the bodily organism, changes and increases elaborateness as the Mason advances to higher stages in the Craft, symbolizing (in theory) the actual development gradually taking place in his nature.

Moreover, as in the outer heavens of nature (the sun, moon, and stars) exist and function, so in the personal heavens of man, there operate metaphysical forces inherent in himself and described by the same terms. In the make-up of each of us exists a psychic magnetic field of various forces, determining our temperaments and tendencies and influencing our future. Those forces have also been named the sun, moon, and planets. The science of their interaction and outworking was the ancient science of astronomy, or, as it is now more often called, astrology. It is one of the liberal arts and sciences recommended to the study of every Mason and the pursuit of which belongs in particular to the Fellowcraft stage.

The Positions of the Officers of the Lodge

The seven Officers—three principal and three subordinate ones, with an additional minor one serving as a connecting link with the outside world—represent seven aspects of consciousness psychologically interactive and coordinated into unity to constitute a "just and perfect lodge." As a person, anyone whose faculties are so disordered or uncoordinated is described as insane, so a lodge would be imperfect and incapacitated for effective work if its functional mechanism were incomplete.

Seven is universally the number of completeness of the periods of creation. The spectrum of light consists of seven colors, the musical scale of seven notes, our division of time into weeks of seven days, and our physiological changes that run in cycles of seven years. Man is a seven-fold organism in correspondence with all these.

When the Master's gavel knocks, those of the Wardens at once repeat the knocks. When the Divine Principle in man speaks in the depth of his being, the remaining portions of his nature should reverberate in sympathy. Without the presence of this Divine Principle in him, man would be less than human. Because of this presence in him, he can become more than human. By cultivating his consciousness of it, he may become unified with it in proportion as he denies and renounces everything in himself that is less than divine. It is the inextinguishable Light of a Master Mason, which, being immortal and eternal, continues to shine when everything temporal and mortal has disappeared.

The Senior Warden, while the Master's chief executive officer, is his antithesis and opposite pole. He personifies the soul, the psychic or animistic principle in man, which, if unassociated with and unillumined by the greater light of the Spirit or Master-principle, has no inherent light. At best, he in the West can but reflect and transmit that greater light from the East, as the moon receives and reflects sunlight. Wherefore, in Masonry, his light is spoken of as the moon. In Nature, when the moon is not shone upon by the sun, it is invisible and virtually non-existent for us; when it is, it is one of the most radiant of phenomena. Similarly, human intelligence is valuable or negligible, depending on whether it is enlightened by the Master Light of the Divine Principle or merely darkly functioning from its unillumined energies. In the former case, it is the chief executive faculty or transmitting medium of the Supreme Wisdom; in the latter, it can display nothing better than brute reason.

Midway between the master light from the East and the "Moon" in the West is placed the Junior Warden in the South, symbolizing the third greater light, the "Sun." Masonically, the "sun" stands for the illuminated human intelligence and understanding, which results from the material brain-mind being thoroughly permeated and enlightened by the Spiritual Principle. It denotes these two in a balanced and harmonious interaction, the Junior Warden personifying the balance point or meeting place of man's natural reason and spiritual intuition. Accordingly, it is he who, as representing this enlightened mental condition, asserts in the Second Degree (which is the degree of personal development where that condition is theoretically achieved) that he has been enabled in that degree to discover a sacred symbol placed in the center of the building. What is meant is that the man who has in reality (and not merely ceremonially) advanced to the second degree of self-development has now discerned that God is not outside him but within him, overshadowing his own "building" or organism. A discovery which he is thereupon urged to follow up with fervor and zeal so that he may more and more closely unify himself with this Divine Principle. However, this process requires time, effort, and self-struggle. Unification is not achieved suddenly. There are obstacles, "enemies" in the way, obstructing it due to the aspirant's imperfections and limitations. These must first be gradually overcome, and the eradication of these is alluded to in the sign of the degree, indicating that he desires to cleanse his heart and cast away all evil from it, to purify himself for a closer alliance with that pure Light. It is only by this "sunlight," this newly found illumination, that he has become able to see into the depths of his nature. This is the "Sun," which, like Joshua, he prays may "stand still" and retain its light until he has conquered all these enemies. The problem of the much-discredited biblical miracle of the sun standing still in the heavens disappears when its true meaning is perceived in the light of the interpretation given by the compilers of the Masonic ritual. They knew well that it was not the solar orb that miraculously stayed in its course in violation of natural law. They knew that the "sun" in question denotes an enlightened perceptive state experienced by everyone who in this "valley of Ajalon" undertakes the task of self-conquest and "fighting the battles of the Lord" against his own lower propensities.

We have now considered the Senior and Junior Wardens in their respective psychological significances, described as the "Moon" and "Sun." In this connection, it is well worth pointing out that the lights of the Moon and Sun become extinguished in the darkness of the Third Degree. In the great work of self-transformation, they are lights and help to a point. When that point is reached, they are of no further avail. The grip of each of them proves a slip. The Master-Light, or Divine Principle, alone takes up and completes the regenerative change: "The sun shall be no more thy light by day, neither for brightness shall the moon give light unto thee; but the Lord shall be unto thee an everlasting light and thy God thy glory, and the days of thy mourning shall be ended." (*Is. lx.* 19-20).

The three lesser Officers and Tyler (which ones depend on the jurisdiction), who complete the executive septenary with the three principal ones, represent the three greater Officers' energies transmitted into the lower faculties of man's organism. The seven thus typify the mechanism of human consciousness. They represent a series of discrete but coordinated parts connecting man's outer nature with his inmost Divine Principle and providing the necessary channels for reciprocal action between his organism's spiritual and material poles.

In other words, and to use an alternative symbol of the same fact, man is potentially a seven-branched golden candlestick. Potentially so, because as yet, he has not transmuted the base metals of his nature into gold or lit up the seven candles or parts of his organism with the Promethean Fire of the Divine Principle. Meanwhile, that symbol of what is possible to him is offered for his reflection and contemplation, and he may profitably study the description of a regenerated, perfected man given in *Revelation* 1, 12-20.

The Greater and Lesser Lights

The purpose of Initiation may be defined as follows: it is to stimulate and awaken the Candidate to direct cognition and irrefutable demonstration of facts and truths of his being about which previously he has been either wholly ignorant or only notionally informed. It is to bring him into direct conscious contact with the Realities underlying the surface images of things so that he is directly and convincingly confronted with Truth instead of merely holding beliefs or opinions about himself, the Universe, and God. Finally, it moves him to become the Good and the Truth, revealed by identifying himself with it. (This is, of course, a gradual process involving greater or less time and effort in proportion to the capacity and equipment of the candidate himself.)

The restoration to Light of the candidate in the First Degree is, therefore, indicative of a significant crisis. It symbolizes the first enlargement of perception that, thanks to his earnest aspirations and the good offices of the guides and instructors to whom he has yielded himself, Initiation brings him. It reveals to him a threefold symbol—the three great though emblematic lights in Masonry—the Holy Bible, Square, and Compasses in a state of conjunction. The two latter resting on the first named as their ground or base. As this triple symbol is the first object that his outward eyes gaze upon after enlightenment, so in correspondence, it is what they emblematize as the first truth his inward eye is meant to recognize and contemplate.

He is also made aware of three emblematic lesser lights, described as alluding to the "Sun," "Moon," and "Master of the Lodge" (the psychological significance of which has already been explained in our interpretation of the Officers of the Lodge).

Now, the candidate can only see the three greater Lights with the help of the three lesser ones. In other words, the lesser triad is the instrument by which he beholds the greater one. It is his perceptive faculty (himself) looking out upon something larger that he has not yet identified.

What is implied, then, is that the lesser lights of the candidate's average finite intelligence are employed to reveal to him the greater lights or fundamental essences of his as yet undeveloped being. An elementary consciousness is made aware of its submerged source and roots and placed in sharp contrast with the limitless possibilities available when those hidden depths have been developed and brought into function. The candidate's problem and destiny is to lose himself to find himself. He is to unify his lesser with his greater lights so that he no longer functions merely with an elementary reflex consciousness but in alliance with the All-Conscious with which he has become identified. In the Royal Arch Degree, he will discover that this identification of the lesser and greater lights has theoretically become achieved. The interlaced triangles of lights surrounding the central altar in that Supreme Degree imply the union of perceptive faculty with the object of their contemplation: the blending of the human and the Divine consciousness.

What do the three Greater Lights emblematize, and what does their intimate conjunction connote?

(1) The written Word is the emblem and external expression of the unwritten Eternal Word, the Logos or Substantial Wisdom of Deity out of which every living soul has emanated and which, therefore, is the ground or base of human life. "In the beginning was the Word and the Word was with God and the Word was God; without Him was not anything made that was made; in Him was life and the life was the light of men; and the light shineth in darkness and the darkness

comprehendeth it not." In an intelligently conducted lodge, the Sacred Volume should lie open at the first chapter of the Gospel by St. John, the patron saint of Masonry. This is done so that these words may meet the candidate's eyes when restored to light and remind him that the basis of his being is the Divine Word resident and shining within his darkness and ignorance. At that point, he does not realize or comprehend that fact. He has lost all consciousness of that truth, and this dereliction is the "lost Word" of which every Mason is theoretically in search. Finding that, he will find all things, for he will have found God within himself. Let the candidate also reflect that the secret motions and promptings of this Word within him have compelled him to enter the Craft and seek initiation into Light. In the words of a great initiate, "thy seeking is the cause of thy finding," for the finding is but the final coming to self-consciousness of that inward force that first compelled the quest for Light. Otherwise, all ceremonial initiation will be without benefit, and he will fail to understand its external symbols and allegories.

(2) The Square, resting upon the Sacred Volume, symbolizes the human soul as it was generated from the Divine Word, which underlies it. That soul was created "square," perfect, and like everything that proceeded from the Creator's hand, it was originally pronounced "very good." However, it was invested with freedom of choice and capacity for error. The builder's square, however, used as a craft symbol, approximates a triangle with its apex downwards and base upwards. It is a very ancient symbol of man's soul and psychic constitution known as the Water Triangle.

(3) The Compasses interlaced with the square symbolize the Spirit of the Soul is functional energy or Fire. Of itself, the soul would be a mere inert passivity, a negative quantity unbalanced by a positive opposite. Its active properties are the product of the union of itself with its underlying and inspiring Divine basis, as modified by the good or evil tendencies of the

soul itself. God "breathed into man the breath of life and man became—no longer a soul, which he was previously—but a *living* (energizing) soul." This product, or fiery energy, of the soul, is the Spirit of man (a good or evil force accordingly as he shapes it) and is symbolized by what has always been known as the Fire Triangle (with the apex upward and base downward). That symbol is approximately reproduced in the Compasses.

To summarize, the three Greater Lights emblematize the inextricably interwoven triadic groundwork of man's being: (1) the Divine Word or Substance as its foundation; (2) a passive soul emanated from that place; (3) an active spirit or energizing capacity generated in the soul as the result of the interaction of the former two. Man, himself, therefore (viewed apart from the temporal body now clothing him) is a triadic unit, rooted in and proceeding from the basic Divine Substance.

Observe that in the First Degree, the points of the Compasses are hidden by the Square. In the Second Degree, one fact is disclosed. In the Third, both are exhibited. The implication is that as the Candidate progresses, the inertia and negativity of the soul become increasingly transmuted and superseded by the positive energy and activity of the Spirit. The Fire Triangle gradually assumes preponderance over the Water Triangle, signifying that the Aspirant becomes more vividly living and spiritually conscious than he was initially.

Opening and Closing the Lodge
First or Entered Apprentice Degree

If the lodge, with its appointments and officers, is a sacramental figure of oneself and of the mechanism of personal consciousness, opening the lodge in successive degrees implies the ability to expand, open, and intensify that consciousness in three distinct stages, surpassing the normal level applicable to ordinary, mundane affairs.

This fact mostly goes unrecognized in Masonic lodges. The openings and closings are regarded as casual formalities devoid of interior purpose or meaning. In contrast, they are ceremonies of the highest instructiveness and rites with a distinctive purpose that should not be violated by casual routine performance or without understanding what they imply.

A flower "opens its lodge" when it unfolds its petals and displays its center to the sun, which vitalizes it. Opening a Masonic lodge is a sacramental way of opening the human mind and heart to God. It is a dramatized form of the psychological processes involved in doing so.

Three degrees or stages of such openings are intricate. First, one appropriate to the apprentice stage of development is a simple *Sursum corda!* or call to "lift up your hearts!" above the everyday level of external things. Second, a more advanced opening, adapted for those who are themselves more advanced in science and capable of greater things than apprentices. This opening is proclaimed "upon the square," which the First Degree opening is not. This implies that it especially involves using the psychic and higher intellectual nature (as previously explained by the Square or Water Triangle). Third, a still more advanced opening is declared to be "upon the center" for those of Master Mason's rank, and it points to an opening up of consciousness to the very center and depths of one's being.

How far and to what degree any of us can open his lodge determines our actual position in Masonry and discloses whether we are, in very fact, Masters, Craftsmen, or Apprentices, or only titularly such. Progress in this, as in other things, comes only with intelligent practice and sustained sincere effort. But what is quite overlooked and desirable to emphasize is the power, as an initiatory force, of *an assemblage* of individuals, each sufficiently progressed and competent to "open his Lodge" in the sense described. Such an assembly, gathered in one place and acting with a common definite purpose, creates, as it were, a vortex in the mental and psychical atmosphere into which a newly initiated candidate is drawn. The tension created by their collective energy of thought and will—progressively intensifying as the lodge is opened in each successive degree and correspondingly relaxing as each degree is closed—acts and leaves a permanent effect upon the candidate (always assuming that he is equally in earnest and "properly prepared" in an interior sense), inducing a favorable mental and spiritual *rapport* between him and those with whom he seeks to be elevated into organic spiritual membership. Further, it both stimulates his perceptivity and causes his mentality to become charged and permeated with the ideas and uplifting influences projected upon him by his initiators.

The fact that a candidate is not admitted within the lodge without certain assurances, safeguards, and tests indicates that peril to the mental and spiritual organism is recognized as attending the presumptuous engaging in the things with which Initiation deals. As the flaming sword is described as keeping the way to the Tree of Life from those yet unfitted to approach it, so does the secret law of the Spirit still avenge itself upon those unqualified to participate in the knowledge of its mysteries. Hence the commandment "Thou shalt not take the name of the Lord thy God in vain," that is, by invoking Divine Energy for unworthy or vain purposes.

Here, and upon the general subject of the signs, tokens, and words employed and communicated in Initiatory Rites, may be quoted the following useful words:

> "The symbols of the Mysteries embodied in the sign of the Square and Circle constitute the eternal language of the gods, the same in all worlds, from all eternity. They have had neither the beginning of years nor the end of days. They are contemporary with time and with eternity. They are the Word of God, the Divine Logos, articulate and expressed in forms of language. Each sign

possesses a corresponding vocal expression, bodily gesture, or mental intention. This fact is of great importance to the student of the Wisdom, for in it rests the main reason for the secrecy and the intense watchfulness and carefulness of the stewards of the Mysteries lest the secret doctrines find expression on the lips or through the action of unfit persons to possess the secrets. The secret power of the Mysteries is within the signs. Any person attaining natural and supernatural states by the process of development, if his heart be untuned and his mind withdrawn from the Divine to the human within him, that power becomes a power of evil instead of a power of good. An unfaithful initiate, in the degree of the Mysteries he has attained, is capable, by his antecedent preparations and processes, of diverting the power to unholy, demoniacal, astral, and dangerous uses [. . .]. Using the signs, vocal sounds, physical acts, and mental intentions was prohibited except under rigorously tested conditions. For instance, the utterance of a symbolical sound or a physical act corresponding to a sign belonging to a given degree in a congregation of an inferior degree was fatal in its effects. No initiates who have not attained that degree are admitted to its congregations in each degree. Only initiates of that degree, and above it, can sustain the pressure of dynamic force generated in the spiritual atmosphere and concentrated in that degree. The actual mental ejaculation of a sign, under such circumstances, brought the immediate putting forth of an occult power corresponding to it. In all the congregations of the initiates, an Inner Guard was stationed within the sanctuary, chancel, or oratory at the entrance door, with the drawn sword in his hand, to ward off unqualified trespassers and intruders. It was no mere formal or metaphorical performance. It was at the risk of the life of

any man attempting to make an entrance if he succeeded in crossing the threshold. Secret signs, passwords, and other tests were applied to all who knocked at the door before admission was granted. The possession of the Mysteries, after initiation, and the use of the signs, either vocally or by action, with "intention" in their use (not as mere mechanical repetition), was attended by occult powers directed to the subjects of their special intention, whether absent or present or for purposes beneficial to the cause in contemplation."
(H. E. Sampson's *Progressive Redemption*, pp. 171-174).

To "open the lodge" and bring it to higher realities is no simple task. Especially for those who have closed and sealed it by their habitual thought modes, preconceptions, and distrust of whatever is not sensibly demonstrable. Yet all these propensities must be eradicated or shut out, and the lodge tyled against them. They have no part or place in the things of the inward man. Effort and practice are also needed to attain stability of mind, control of emotion and thought, and to acquire interior stillness and the harmony of all our parts. As the formal ceremony of lodge opening is achieved only by the organized cooperation of its constituent officers, the due opening of our inner man to God can only be accomplished by the consensus of all our parts and faculties. The absence or failure of any part invalidates the whole. The W.M. alone cannot open the lodge; he can only invite his brethren to assist him through a concerted process and the unified wills of his subordinates. So, too, with opening the lodge of man's soul. His spiritual will, as master faculty, summons his other faculties to assist it; he "sees that none but Masons are present" by taking care that his thoughts and motives in approaching God are pure. He calls all these "brethren" in order to prove their due qualification for the work in hand. Only then, after seeing that the lodge is properly formed, does he undertake the responsibility of invoking the descent of the Divine blessing and influx upon the unified and dedicated whole.

Of all which the Psalmist writes: "How good and joyful a thing it is for brethren to dwell together in unity. . .. It is like the precious ointment (anointing) which flows down unto the skirts of the clothing." This implies that the Divine influx, when it descends in response to such an invocation, floods and illuminates the entire human organism, even its carnal sense-extremities (the "skirts of the clothing" of the soul). Also compare the Christian Master's words: "When thou prayest, enter into thy secret chamber (the lodge of the soul), and when thou hast shut thy door (by tyling the mind to all outward concerns and thoughts), pray to the Father who seeth in secret, who shall reward thee openly" (by conscious communion).

The previous may help to interpret the meaning and purpose of the Opening in the First Degree and to indicate the conditions and spiritual atmosphere that ought to exist when a Lodge is open for business in that degree. Suppose the lodge opening is a real opening and not a mere ceremonial form. In that case, it will be apparent at once that they are deeply moving a candidate who enters them seeking initiation and spiritual advancement. Suppose he is a worthy candidate, properly prepared in his heart and an earnest seeker for the light. In that case, the mere fact of his entering such an atmosphere will impress and awaken his dormant soul faculties, which constitute an initiation and an indelible memory. On the other hand, if he is an unworthy or poorly prepared candidate, that atmosphere and those conditions will prove repellent to him, and he will be the first to wish to withdraw and not repeat the experience.

The Closing of the First Degree implies the reverse process of the Opening, the relaxing of the inward energies, and the return of the mind to its former habitual level. Yet not without gratitude expressed for Divine favors and perceptions received during the period of openness. Nor without counsel to keep closed the book of the heart and lay aside the use of its jewels until we are duly called to resume them. Since silence and secrecy are essential to the gestation and growth of the inward man. "He who has seen God is dumb."

Second or Fellowcraft Degree

Opening the Second Degree presupposes an ability to open the inner nature and consciousness to a much more advanced stage than is possible for the beginner. The beginner, in theory, is supposed to undergo a long period of discipline and apprenticeship in the elementary work of self-preparation and be able to satisfy specific tests that he has done so before being qualified for advancement to the Fellowcraft stage of self-building.

Again, that opening may be a personal work for the individual Mason or a collective work in an assembly of Fellowcrafts and superior Masons to pass an Apprentice to Fellowcraft rank.

The word admitting the qualified Apprentice to a Fellow-craft lodge is significant and ordinarily passes without any observation or understanding of its propriety. It is said to denote "in plenty" and to be illustrated by an "ear of corn near to a fall of water" (which two objects are the meaning of the Hebrew word in question). This describes the candidate and his spiritual condition. He is like an ear of corn planted near and nourished by a fall of water. As achieved in the Apprentice stage, his spiritual growth is typified by the ripening corn; the fertilizing cause of its growth is the down-pouring upon his inner nature of the revivifying dew of heaven resulting from his aspiration towards the light.

The work appropriated to the Apprentice Degree is gaining purity and control of his grosser nature, its appetites and affections. It is symbolized by working the rough ashlar dug from the quarry into due shape for building purposes. The "quarry" is the undifferentiated raw material or group soul of humanity from which he has issued into individuated existence.

The apprentice work relates to the conquest of the sense-nature and its propensities. Once achieved, the next stage is the development and control of the intellectual nature. This is the investigation of the "hidden paths of nature (*i.e.*, the human psychological nature) and science" (the *gnosis* of self-knowledge).

It should be noted that the candidate is told that he is now "*permitted* to extend his research" into these hidden paths. If this work is undertaken before the purifications of the Apprentice stage have been accomplished, the candidate's mentality is perilous. Hence, permission is not given until the preliminary task has been done and duly tested.

The Second Degree's work is a purely philosophical work involving deep psychological self-analysis. The experience of unusual phenomena as the psychic faculties of the soul begin to unfold themselves, and the anxiety of abstract Truth (formerly described as mathematics) begins. This work is beyond the average modern Mason's mental horizon and capacity. However, in the Mysteries of Antiquity, the *Mathesis* (or mental discipline) was an outstanding feature that produced the intellectual giants of Greek philosophy. Hence, today, the degree is dull and uninteresting since psychic experience and intellectual principles cannot be spectacular and dramatic.

Our ancient brethren of this degree met in the porchway of King Solomon's Temple. This is a way of saying that natural philosophy is the porchway to the attainment of Divine Wisdom. It meant the study of man leads to knowledge of God by revealing to man the ultimate divinity at the base of human nature. This study or self-analysis of human nature is earth-measuring, probing, sounding, and determining our organism's limits, proportions, and potentialities in its physical and psychical aspects. The ordinary natural consciousness is directed outwards, perceives only outward objects, and thinks only of an outward Deity separate and away from us. It can accordingly know only shadows, images, and illusions. The science of the Mysteries directs that that process must be reversed. It says: "Just as you have symbolically shut and closely tyled the door of your lodge against all outsiders, so you must shut out all perception of outward images, all desire for external things and material welfare, and turn your consciousness and aspirations wholly inward. The Vital and Immortal Principle — the Kingdom of Heaven — is within you, not to be found outside you. Like the prodigal son in the parable, you have wandered away from it into a far country and lost all consciousness of it. You have come down and down, as by a spiral motion or a winding staircase, into this lower world and imperfect form of existence, coiling around you as you came increasingly thickening vestures, closing in your outermost dense body of flesh. At the same time, your mentality has woven about you veil after veil of illusory notions concerning your real nature and the nature of true Life. Now, the time and the impulse have finally come for you to return to that inward world. Therefore, reverse your steps. Look no longer outwards but inwards. Go back up that same winding staircase. It will bring you to the Center of Life and *Sanctum Sanctorum* from which you have wandered."

When the Psalmist writes, "Who will go up the hill of the Lord? Even he that hath clean hands and a pure heart," the meaning is identical to what is implied in the ascent of the inwardly "winding staircase" of the Second Degree. Preliminary purification of the mind is essential to its rising to purer realms of being and loftier conscious states than it has been accustomed to. If "the secrets of nature and the principles of intellectual truth" are to become revealed to its view, as the degree intends and promises, the mentality must not be fettered by mundane interests or carnal passions. Suppose it is to "contemplate its intellectual faculties and trace them from their development" until they are found to "lead to the throne of God Himself" and to be rooted in Deity. In that case, it must discard all its former thought habits, prejudices, and preconceptions and be prepared to receive humbly the illumination that will flood into it from the Light of Divine Wisdom.

For the student determined to be mentally disciplined by the Second Degree, the two most instructive sources of information and examples of personal experience may be recommended. One is the Dialogues of Plato and the writings of Plotinus and other Neo-Platonists. The other is the records of the classical Christian contemplatives, such as Eckhart or Ruysbroeck or the "Interior Castle" of St. Theresa. The *Phædrus* of Plato, in particular, is an important record by an initiate of the ancient Mysteries of the psychological experiences referred to in the Fellow-Craft Degree.

The sign of the degree is equivalent to a prayer that the sunlight of that exalted state may "stand still" and persist in us until we have begun the overthrow of all our "enemies" and eradicated all obstacles to our union with that Principle.

The reference to our ancient brethren receiving their wages at the porchway of the Temple of Wisdom is an allusion to an experience common to everyone in the Fellow-Craft stage of development. He learns that old scores due by him to his fellowmen must be paid off and old wrongs righted. He receives the wages of past sins recorded upon his subconsciousness by that pencil that observes and records all our thoughts, words, and actions. The candidate leading the philosophical life realizes he is justly entitled to those wages and receives them without scruple or diffidence. He knows he is justly entitled to them and is only too glad to expiate and purge himself of old offenses. We are all debtors to someone or another for our present position in life. We must repay what we owe to humanity — perhaps with tears or adversity — before we straighten our account with that eternal Justice with which we aspire to become allied.

Third, or Master Mason's Degree

Before dealing with the opening and closing of the Third Degree, it should be observed that in the lodge symbolism, the teaching of the First and Second Degrees is carried forward into the Third. The traditional Tracing Board of the Third Degree exhibits in combination (1) the checkered floor-work, (2) the two pillars at the porchway of the Temple, (3) the winding staircase, and (4) a dormer window above the porchway. The brief explanation is given that the checker-work is for the High Priest to walk upon, and the dormer window is that which gave light to it. The entire symbol is but one comprehensive glyph or pictorial diagram of the condition of a candidate aspiring to Master Mason's rank. As the temple's high priest, he must have his bodily nature and its varied desires underfoot. He must have developed strength of will and character to "walk upon" this checker-work and withstand its appeals. He must also be able to ascend the winding staircase of his inner nature, educate and habituate his mentality to higher conscious states, and establish that he will be unaffected by seductive or affrighting perceptions that may meet him. By the cultivation of this "strength" and the ability to "establish" himself upon the loftier conscious levels, he coordinates the two pillars at the porchway of his inmost sanctuary—namely, the physical and psychical supports of his organism—and acquires the "stability" involved in regeneration and requisite to him before passing on to "that last and greatest trial" which awaits him. "In strength will I establish My house that it may stand firm." Man's perfected organism is what is meant by "My house." It was the same organism and stability that the Christian Master spoke of in saying, "Upon this rock will I build my church, and the gates of the underworld shall not prevail against it."

During all the discipline and labor involved in attaining this stability, there has shone a light on the path from the first moment that his Apprentice's vision was opened to a larger truth, light from the science and philosophy of the Order itself, which is proving his "porchway" to the ultimate sanctuary within.

But now the last and greatest trial of his fortitude and fidelity, one imposing a still more serious obligation of endurance, awaits him. Although guided by that light, he has progressed by his natural powers and efforts. Now, the time has come for those props to be removed and for all reliance upon natural abilities, self-will, and normal rational understanding to be surrendered. The aspirant must abandon himself utterly to the transformative action of his Vital and Immortal Principle alone, passively suffering it to complete the work in entire independence of his lesser faculties. He must "lose his life to save it." He must surrender all he has felt to be his life to find a life of an altogether higher order.

Hence, the Third Degree is that of mystical death, of which bodily death is symbolic. Just as physical birth is taken in the First Degree as a symbolic entrance upon the path of regeneration. In all the mystery systems of the past, this degree of mystical death will be found to be an outstanding and essential feature before the final stage of perfection or regeneration. As an illustration, one has only to refer to a sectional diagram of the Great Pyramid of Egypt, which was constructed not to be merely a temple of initiation but to record in permanent form the principles upon which regeneration is attainable. Its entrance passage extends for some distance into the building as a narrow ascending channel through which the postulant who desires to reach the center must creep in no small discomfort and restrictedness. This was to emblematize the discipline and up-hill labor of self-purification requisite in the Apprentice Degree. At a certain point, this restricted passage opens into a long and lofty gallery, still upon a steeply rising gradient, up which the postulant had to pass, but in a condition of ease and liberty. This symbolized the condition of illumination and expanded intellectual liberty associated with the Fellow-craft Degree. It ended at a place where the candidate once more had to force his way on hands and knees through the smallest aperture of all. It led to the central chamber, which stood and still stands the great sarcophagus where he was placed and underwent the last supreme ordeal. He was raised from the dead, initiated, and perfected.

The word of admission communicated to the candidate for the Third Degree is noteworthy, as is the reason for it. It is a Hebrew name said to be that of the first artificer in metals and "in worldly possessions." Now, it will be evident that the name of the first man who worked at metal-making in the ordinary sense can be of no interest or concern to us today, nor has the information the slightest bearing upon human regeneration. It is a veil of allegory concealing some relevant truth. Such it will be found to be upon recognizing that Hebrew Biblical names often represent not persons, but personifications of spiritual principles and that Biblical history is not an ordinary history of temporal events but a record of eternally true spiritual facts. The matter is, therefore, interpretable as follows: We know from the teaching of the Entered Apprentice Degree what "money and metals" are in the Masonic sense and that they represent the attractive power of temporal possessions and earthly belongings and affections of whatever description. We know too that from the attraction and seductiveness of these things, and even from the desire for them, it is essential to be free if one desires to attain that Light and those riches of Wisdom for which the candidate professes. Not that he must become literally and physically dispossessed of worldly possessions, but he must be so utterly detached from them that he cares not whether he owns any or not and is content, if need be, to be divested of them entirely if they stand in the way of his finding "treasure in heaven." His initiation into anything should be deferred as long as he clings to worldly possessions, or they exercise control over him.

It follows then that it is the personal soul of the candidate himself, which is the "artificer in metals" referred to and which, during the whole of its physical existence, has been engaged in trading with "metals." The desire for worldly possessions, sensation, and experience in this outward world of good and evil brought the soul into this world. There, it has woven its present body of flesh around itself, every desire and thought being an "artificer," adding something to or modifying its natural encasement. The Greek philosophers used to teach that souls secrete their bodies as a snail secretes his shell, and our poet Spenser wrote:

"For of the soul the body form doth take,
 And the soul is formed and doth the body make."

If, then, desire for physical experience and material things brought the soul into material conditions (as is also indicated in the great parable of the Prodigal Son), the relinquishing of that desire is the first necessary step to ensure its return to the condition whence it first emanated. Satiation with and consequent disgust at the "husks" of things instigated the Prodigal Son to aspire to return home. Similar repletion and revolt drive many men to lose all desire for external things and seek peace within themselves, and then redirect their energies in quest of abiding and tangible possessions. This is the moment of his true "conversion" and when he is ripe for initiation into the hidden Mysteries of his being. The First and Second Degrees of Masonry imply that the candidate has undergone lengthy discipline in renouncing external things and cultivating a desire for those within.

But notwithstanding that, he has passed through all the discipline of those Degrees, he is represented at the end of them as being still not entirely purified and to be still "in worldly possessions" in the sense that a residue of attraction by them and reliance upon himself lingers in his heart. These last subtle close-clinging elements of "base metal" in him need to be eradicated if perfection is to be attained. The ingrained defects and tendencies of the soul as the result of all its past habits and experiences are not suddenly eliminated or easily subdued. Self-will and pride are very subtle and may continue to deceive their victim long after he has purged himself of grosser faults. As Cain was the murderer of Abel, so every taint of base metal in oneself debases the gold of the Vital and Immortal Principle. It must be renounced, died too, and transmuted in the crucial process of the Third Degree. Hence, the candidate is entrusted with a name that designates himself at this stage, which indicates that he is still "in worldly possessions." That is some residue of the spirit of this world yet lingers in him, which it is necessary to eliminate from his nature before he can be raised to the sublime degree of Master.

Examination of the text of the opening and closing of the lodge in the Third Degree discloses the philosophy upon which the Masonic system is reared. It indicates that the human soul has originated in the eternal East—that "East" being referable to the world of Spirit and not to any geographical direction—and that thence it has directed its course towards the "West"—the material world which is the antipodes of the spiritual and into which the soul has wandered. Its purpose in so journeying from spiritual to physical conditions is declared to be the quest and recovery of something it has lost, but which, by its industry and suitable instruction, it hopes to find. From this, the loss occurred before its descent into this world. Otherwise, that descent would not have been necessary. What has been lost is not explicitly declared but is implied and is stated to form "the genuine secrets of a Master Mason." It is the loss of a word, or instead of The Word, the Divine Logos, or the basic root and essence of our being. In other words, the soul of man has ceased to be God-conscious and has degenerated into the limited terrestrial consciousness of the ordinary human being. It is in the condition spoken of in the cosmic parable of Adam when extruded from Eden, an exile from the Divine Presence and condemned to toil and trouble. The Wardens declare the quest after this lost Word to have been so far abortive and to have resulted in the discovery, not of that Reality, but of substitutional images of it. All of which implies that, in the strength of merely his natural temporal intelligence, man can find and know nothing more in this world than shadows, images, and phenomenal forms of realities that abide eternally and noumenally in the world of Spirit to which his temporal faculties are at present closed.

Yet, there remains a way of regaining consciousness of that higher world and life. It is by bringing into function a now dormant and submerged faculty resident at the depth and center of his being. That dormant faculty is the Vital and Immortal Principle, which exists as the central point of the circle of his individuality. As the outward Universe is the externalized projection of an indwelling intrinsic Deity, so is the outward individual man the externalization and diffusion of an inherent Divine spark, albeit perverted and distorted by personal self-will and desire. Recover contact with that central Divine Principle by a voluntary renunciation of the intervening obstructions and inharmonious elements in oneself, and man at once ceases to be merely the rationalized animal. He now is and becomes grafted upon a new and Divine life principle, a sharer of Omniscience and a co-operator with Deity. He recovers the lost and genuine secrets of his being and is forever finished with substitutions, shadows, and the representations of reality. He reaches a point and lives from a center from which no Master Mason can ever err or will ever again desire to err, for it is the end, object, and goal of his existence.

Meanwhile, until actual recovery of that lost secret, man must put up with its substitutions and regard these as sacramental of concealed realities, contact with which will be his great reward if he submits himself to the conditions upon which alone he may discover them. Masonry teaches the existence of those realities and the routine essential to their enjoyment as they have been by every other initiatory Order of the past. It is for the fact that this knowledge is and always has been conserved in the world to be ever available for earnest aspirants towards it that gratitude is expressed to the Grand Master of all for having never left Himself or the way of return to Him, without witness in this outer world.

As much has been said about the ceremony of the Third Degree in other papers, it is unnecessary to expound on it further. It may be stated, however, that it alone concludes the Masonic Initiation. The First and Second Degrees are preparatory stages leading up to full Initiation; they are not the Initiation itself. They prescribe the purification of the bodily and mental nature necessary to qualify the candidate for the end, which crowns the whole work. To those unacquainted with what is involved in actual, as distinct from merely ceremonial initiation, and who have no notion of what initiation meant in the old schools of Wisdom, it is nearly impossible to convey any idea of its process or its results. However, despite being high in titular rank, the modern Mason is as little qualified to understand the subject as the man who has never entered a lodge. "To become initiated (or perfected)," says an old authority, Plutarch, "involves dying" but not physical death. This speaks of a moral way of dying in which the soul is loosened from the body and the sensitive life and becomes temporarily detached from being set free to enter the world of Eternal Light and Immortal Being. After most drastic preliminary disciplines, this was achieved in a state of trance and under the supervision of duly qualified Masters and Adepts. They would admit the candidate's liberated soul into its interior principles until it finally reached the Blazing Star or Glory at its own Center. The candidate's soul was then in the light of which it knew itself and God simultaneously. He realized their unity and the "points of fellowship" between them. Then it was that, from this at once awful and sublime experience, the initiated soul was brought back to its bodily encasement again and "reunited to the companions of its former toils" to resume its temporal life, with the conscious realization of Life Eternal superadded to its knowledge and its powers. Only then was it entitled to the name of Master Mason. Only then could it exclaim, in the words of another initiate (Empedocles), "Farewell, all earthly allies; henceforth am I no mortal creature, but an immortal angel, ascending into Divinity and reflecting upon that likeness of it which I have found in myself."

The "secrets" of Freemasonry and initiation are largely connected with this process of introversion of the soul to its own Center. Beyond this brief reference, it is unwise to say more. But in confirmation of what has been indicated, it may be helpful to refer to the 23rd Psalm, in which the Hebrew Initiates speak of the supreme experience of being passed through "the valley of the shadow of death" and the preliminary phases of mental preparation for that ordeal. Stripping that familiar Psalm of the gorgeous metaphor given it in the beautiful Biblical translation, its real meaning may be paraphrased and explained for Masonic students as follows:

"The Vital and Immortal Principle within me is my Initiator and is all-sufficient to lead me to God.

It has made me lie down (in self-discipline and humiliation) in "green pastures" of meditation and mental sustenance.

It has led me beside "still waters" of contemplation (as distinct from the "rough sea of passion" of my natural self).

It is restoring my soul (reintegrating it from chaos and disorder).

Even when I come to pass through the valley of deadly gloom (my interior veils of darkness)

I will fear no evil, for it is with me (as a guiding star); its directions and disciplines will safeguard me.

It provides me with the means of overcoming my inner enemies and weaknesses; It anoints my intelligence with the oil of wisdom; the cup of my mind brims over with new light and consciousness.

Divine Love and Truth, which I shall find face to face at my center, will be a conscious presence to me all the days of my temporal life; thereafter, I shall dwell in a "house of the Lord" (a glorified spiritual body) forever."

The Third Degree is completed and can only be more fully expounded upon by referencing the Holy Royal Arch Ceremony. Therefore, a separate paper will be devoted to that Ceremony.

The Masonic Apron

From what has been said in these pages, the full significance of the Apron will now be perceived and may be summarized thus:

1. The Apron symbolizes the corporeal vesture and condition of the soul (not so much of the temporal physical body as of its permanent invisible corporeity, which will survive the death of the mortal part).

2. The soul fabricates its own body or "apron" by its own desires and thoughts (see *Genesis III*, 7, "They made themselves aprons"), and as these are pure or impure, so will that body be correspondingly transparent and white or dense and opaque.

3. The Senior Warden, as the Master's delegate for that purpose, inaugurates the candidate with the apron in each degree to teach this truth. The Senior Warden represents the soul, which, by its own spirituality, automatically clothes itself

with its own self-made vesture in a way that marks its progress or regress.

4. The unadorned white Apron of the First Degree indicates the purity of soul contemplated as being attained in that degree.

5. The pale blue rosettes added to the Apron in the Second Degree indicate progress in the science of regeneration and that the candidate's spirituality is beginning to develop and blossom. Blue, the color of the sky, is traditionally associated with devotion to spiritual concerns.

6. In the Third Degree, further progress is still emphasized by the increased blue adornments of the Apron, as well as by its silver tassels and the silver serpent used to fasten the apron strings. In the First and Second Degrees, no metal appeared on the Apron. The candidate has been theoretically divesting himself of all base metals and transmuting them into spiritual riches. With Mastership, he has attained an influx of those riches under the emblem of the tassels of silver, a colorless precious metal always associated with the soul, as gold, because of its supreme value and warm color, is associated with Spirit. The silver serpent is the emblem of Divine Wisdom, knitting the soul's new-made vesture together.

7. The pale blue and silver of the Master Mason's Apron intensify in the deep blue and gold ornamentation worn by the Grand Lodge Officers, who, in theory, have evolved to deeper spirituality and transmuted themselves from silver into fine gold. "The king's daughter (the soul) is all glorious within; her clothing is of wrought gold," *i.e.,* wrought or fabricated by her spiritual energies.

A Prayer at Lodge Closing

O Sovereign and Most Worshipful of all Masters, who, in Thy infinite love and wisdom, hast devised our Order as a means to draw Thy children nearer Thee, and hast so ordained its Officers that they are emblems of Thy sevenfold power;

Be Thou unto us an Outer Guard, and defend us from the perils that beset us when we turn from that which is without to that which is within;

Be Thou unto us an Inner Guard, and preserve our souls that desire to pass within the portal of Thy holy mysteries;

Be unto us the Younger Deacon, and teach our wayward feet the true and certain steps upon the path that leads to Thee: Be Thou also the Elder Deacon, and guide us up the steep and winding stairway to Thy throne;

Be unto us the Lesser Warden, and in the meridian sunlight of our understanding speak to us in sacraments that shall declare the splendors of Thy unmanifested light;

Be Thou also unto us the Greater Warden, and in the awful hour of disappearing light, when vision fails, and thought has no more strength, be with us still, revealing to us, as we may bear them, the hidden mysteries of Thy shadow;

And so, through light and darkness, raise us, Great Master, till we are made one with Thee, in the unspeakable glory of Thy presence in the East.

So mote it be.

CHAPTER IV.
The Holy Royal Arch of Jerusalem

UNDER the English Constitution, Freemasonry reaches its climax and conclusion in the Order of the Holy Royal Arch. Various other degrees branch out from the Masonic system's main stem, which either elaborates side-points of its doctrine or re-expresses its teachings in alternative symbolism. These, while of greater or less merit and interest, are beyond our present consideration and, indeed, are superfluities tending rather to diffuse the student's attention than to deepen his insight into the central purpose of the Craft. The taking of additional higher degrees may be indulged in almost indefinitely, but to what purpose if the initial ones, which contain all necessary for understanding the subject, remain imperfectly assimilated? It is a fallacy to suppose that multiplying degrees will result in discovering important arcane secrets that one has failed to find in the rites of the Craft and the Royal Arch. The higher degrees indeed illustrate truths of much interest and often set forth with impressive ceremonial beauty, the appreciation of which will be the greater after, and not before, the meaning of the preliminary ones has been thoroughly absorbed. At the same time, the pursuit of "secrets" is sure to prove deceptive, for the only secrets worth the name or the finding are those incommunicable ones that discover themselves within the personal consciousness of the seeker.

It was accordingly a sound instinct that prompted those who settled the present constitution of the Order to exclude these supplementary refinements and to declare that "Masonry consists of the three Craft Degrees and the Holy Royal Arch and no more." For within that compass is exhibited, or at least outlined, the entire process of human regeneration. So, that after the Royal Arch there really remains nothing more to be said, although what has been said is of course capable of elaboration. The completeness of regeneration theoretically postulated in those four stages is marked, it should be observed, by the very significant expression used in connection with a Royal Arch Chapter, which is interpreted as meaning "My people having obtained mercy." This, in further analysis, signifies that all the parts and faculties ("people") of the candidate's organism have at last become sublimated and integrated in a new quality and higher order of life than that previously enjoyed in virtue of his merely temporal nature. In a word, he has become regenerated. He has achieved the miracle of "squaring the circle" — a metaphorical expression for regeneration, as shall be explained presently.

Although an expansion and completion of the Third Degree, of which it once formed part, there were good reasons for detaching the Royal Arch portion from what now forms the Degree of Master Mason. The two parts, in combination, made an inconveniently long rite. At the same time, a change in the symbolic appointments and officers of the temple of initiation was necessary, as the ceremony proceeded, to give appropriate spectacular representation to the further points calling for expression. Despite this re-arrangement, the Royal Arch is the natural conclusion and fulfillment of the Third Degree. The latter teaches the necessity of mystical death and dramatizes the process of such death and the revival of the newness of life. The Royal Arch carries the process further, showing its fulfillment in the "exaltation" or apotheosis of him who has undergone it. The Master Mason's Degree might be said to be represented in terms of Christian theology by the formula "He suffered and was buried and rose again," while the equivalent of the exaltation ceremony is "He ascended into heaven."

The Royal Arch Degree seeks to express that new and intensified life to which the candidate can be raised and the exalted degree of consciousness that comes with it. From being conscious merely as a natural man and in the naturally restricted way common to everyone born into this world, he becomes exalted (while still in his natural flesh) to consciousness in a uncanny and limitless way. As has been said in previous papers, all initiation aims to lift human consciousness from lower to higher levels by quickening the latent spiritual potentialities in man to their full extent through appropriate discipline. And that being the level the Order of the Royal Arch treats ceremonially, it follows that this system of Masonry as a sacramental system reaches its climax and conclusion in that Order.

As has also been already shown, to attain that level involves as its essential prerequisite the total refrainment, renouncement, and renovation of one's original nature. It calls for the surrender of one's natural desires, tendencies, and preconceptions. It also demands the abandonment and nullifying of one's natural self-will, by such a habitual discipline and self-denial and gradual but vigorous opposition to all these as will cause them gradually to atrophy and die down. "He that loves his life shall lose it, and he that hates his life in this world shall keep it unto life eternal. Except a corn of wheat falls into the ground and dies, it abides alone. But if it dies, it bringeth forth much fruit." As with a seed of wheat, so with man. Suppose he persists in clinging to the present natural life he knows. If he refuses to recognize that a higher quality of life is possible for him or is unwilling to make the necessary effort to attain it, he "abides alone," gets nowhere, and only frustrates his spiritual evolution. But if he is willing to "die" in the sense indicated, if he will so re-orientate his will and silence his natural energies and desires as to give the Vital and Immortal Principle within him the chance to assert itself and supersede them, then from the disintegrated material of his old nature that germ of true life will spring into growth in him and bear much fruit. By the stepping-stones of initiation, he will rise from his death to higher things than he can otherwise experience.

This necessity of self-dying — *not*, we repeat, the physical death of the body but a mystical death-in-life of everything except the body — is the first and fundamental fact to be grasped before one may hope to realize or even to understand the mystery of the Royal Arch Degree. *"Mors janua vitae."* Death to self is the portal to true life. There is no other way. It is the inescapable law and condition of the soul's progress.

But since it is a process involving a "most serious trial of fortitude and fidelity" and a grapple with oneself from which the timorous and self-diffident may well shrink, the Mystery systems have always exhibited an example for the instruction, encouragement, and emulation of those prepared to make the attempt and the necessary sacrifice. To inspire them to the task, the Initiatory Colleges have held up a prototype of the person of some great soul who has already trodden the same path and emerged triumphant. It matters nothing whether the prototype is one whose historical actuality and identity can be demonstrated or whether he can be regarded only as legendary or mythical. The point is not merely teaching historical facts but enforcing a spiritual principle. In Egypt, the prototype was Osiris, who was slain by his malignant brother Typhon. Osiris' mangled limbs were collected in a coffer from which he emerged, reintegrated, and divinized. In Greece, the prototype was Bacchus, torn to pieces by the Titans. Baldur in Scandinavia and Mithra in Græco-Roman Europe were similar prototypes. In Masonry, the prototype is Hiram Abiff, who met his death due to a conspiracy by a crowd of workmen of whom there were three principal ruffians. In the Christian and chief of all systems, since it comprehends and re-expresses all the others, the greatest of the Exemplars died at the hands of the mob, headed also by three chief ruffians, Judas, Caiaphas, and Pilate. Suppose in Masonry, the mystical death is dramatized more realistically than the resurrection that follows upon it. In that case, that resurrection is nevertheless shown in the "raising" of the candidate to the rank of Master Mason and his "reunion with the companions of former toils." This implies the reintegration and resumption of all his old faculties and powers in a sublimated state, just as the limbs of the risen Osiris were said to reunite into a new whole and as the Christian Master withdrew His mutilated body from the tomb and reassumed it, transmuted into one of supernatural substance and splendor.

Therefore, we must now consider how the Royal Arch Degree exhibits the attainment of a new order of life. But it may be as well to say in advance that for those who are not normally looking beyond surface values and material meanings, it is likely to present some difficulty of comprehension and acceptance. The Royal Arch, however, would not be the Supreme Degree of this Masonic System if it did not move upon a supremely high level of thought and instruction. It was not compiled to accommodate the elementary intelligence theoretically characterizing the philosophically untrained neophyte. It presupposes that its candidate has passed through a long, strenuous period of purification and mental discipline, during which his understanding has widened and deepened. At the same time, his fidelity to the inward Light, which has conducted him safely so far, has induced in him humility and docility fitting him for what still awaits him — the attainment of that Wisdom that is concealed from this world's wise and prudent but is revealed unto babes. It is a rite of initiation dealing less with his gross human nature and his ordinary temporal mentality (the subject of purification of the earlier degrees) than with, the higher reaches and possibilities of his understanding and consciousness. As it is, what can be said here can, at best, be but a partial and incomplete exposition of a theme calling instead for disciplined imagination and reverent reflection than for reasoned argument. Certain things must be omitted entirely from the explanation. In contrast, others are mentioned with hesitancy and at the risk of being misunderstood or rejected by others who do not yet realize that in these matters, "the letter killeth, the spirit vivifies" and that "spiritual truths must be spiritually discerned."

Before interpreting the ceremony itself, it is desirable to indicate four noteworthy features connected with this Order and distinguish them from the three grades leading to it. Even if these are incidentals, the difficulties of both exposition and apprehension will already make themselves felt.

First, no one can be received into a Chapter without first attaining Master Mason's rank.

Second, the circular symbol of the Grand Geometrician, which in the Second Degree shone high above the ceiling of the Temple and in the Third Degree, had moved downwards and burned as a glimmering ray in the East to guide the candidate's feet into the way of peace, has now entirely descended to the checker-work floor, where it rests as the center and cubical focus of the entire organism and bears the Sacred and Ineffable Name, as also those of Solomon and the two Hirams.

Third, the Assembly's constitution no longer consists of seven officers but nine, who are grouped into three triads about the Central Sacred Symbol.

Fourth, the Assembly, regarded as a unity, is no longer designated a Lodge but a Chapter.

The first of these points — that none but a Master Mason can enter the Royal Arch — has already been accounted for. It is not feasible, nor is it within the law governing the process of spiritual evolution, for any who has not experienced the stage of mystical death to have experience of that which lies beyond that death. As an unborn physical infant can know nothing of this world, in which nevertheless it exists until initiated into it by birth, so the embryonic spiritual child cannot be born into conscious function upon the plane of the Spirit until it has become entirely detached from the enfolding carnal matrix and tendencies to which it has been habituated. The second and third points can be considered together. The re-arrangement of the factors constituting the ceremonial temple is symbolic of a structural re-arrangement in the candidate's psychical organization. This has undergone a repolarization as the result of the descent into it of that high central Light which at first but shone as it were in his "heavens," afar off and above him, illumining the dormer window of his natural intelligence. Consider deeply what this change implies. The Day-star from on high has now visited him; the fontal source of all consciousness has descended into the very checker-work material of his transient physical organism, not merely permeating it temporarily with light but taking root and becoming grafted there substantially and permanently. In theological language, God has become man, and man has become divinized by this descent and union. In Masonic terms, the candidate's Vital and Immortal Principle resident has finally superseded his temporal life principle and established him upon a new center of incorruptible life. Now, and perhaps only now, the necessity for the earlier purifications, discipline, self-crucifixion, and death of all the lower nature becomes thoroughly appreciable. How could the purity of the Divine Essence tabernacle be in the coarse body of the sensualist? How could Eternal Wisdom unfold its treasures in a mind unenlightened or caring only for base metals and material pursuits? How could the Universal Will cooperate with and function through the man whose petty personal will blocks its channel, antagonizing it at every turn with his selfish preferences and disordered desires? A Master Mason, then, in the complete sense of the term, is no longer an ordinary man but a divinized man, one in whom the Universal and the personal consciousness have come into union. Such an individual's quality of life and consciousness must differ vastly from other men's. His whole being is different and geared towards another center. That new center is described Grand Geometrician of man's universe since its action upon the organism of whoever surrenders himself to its influence causes a redisposition of functional and conscious faculty. The knowledge of this fact was with the wise ancients, original science of Geometry (literally "earth-measuring;" determining the occult potentialities of the earth or temporal organism under spiritual stresses). "God geometrizes," wrote Plato, with intimate knowledge of the subject. Many of the Euclidean and Pythagorean theorems, now regarded merely as mathematical demonstrations, were originally expressions, veiled in mathematical glyphs, of the esoteric science of soul-building or proper Masonry. The well-known 47th Proposition of the First Book of Euclid is an example of this and, in consequence, has come (though few modern Masons could explain why) to be inscribed upon the Past Master's official jewel. Again, the squaring of the circle — that problem which has baffled so many modern mathematicians — is an occult expression signifying that Deity, symbolized by the all-containing circle, has attained form and manifestation in a "square" or human soul. It expresses the mystery of the Incarnation, accomplished within the personal soul.

Under the stress of the Geometrizing Principle now found symbolically integrated within the candidate's temporal organism, a re-distribution of his component powers has become effected. His repolarized condition is symbolized by an equilateral triangle with a point at its center, and such a triangle will be found, worked in gold, upon the sash worn by the Companions of the Order. The significance of this triangle is that the tripartite aspects of him who wears it (that is, the spiritual, psychical, and physical parts of him) now stand equalized and equilibrated around their common Life-Principle at the center, fitted and equipped for Its purpose. Yet each of these three divisions, though unitary, is philosophically triadic in composition when subjected to intellectual analysis. "Every monad is the parent of a triad" is another maxim of the Ancients, who anticipated the modern Hegelian proposition of metaphysics that thesis, antithesis, and synthesis are the essential ingredients of a given truth. Hence, it comes about that the three aspects of each of the three sides of our equilateral triangle are ceremonially personified by the nine officers of the

Chapter—three in the East representing the spiritual side, three in the West figuring the soul or psychical side, and three subordinate links connecting these other two. (These will be further and more conveniently treated later when the symbolic nature of the officers is dealt with).

The fourth point to be noticed was the designation change from "Lodge" to "Chapter." The word "Chapter" derives from *Caput*, or "head." However, the reason for the name change lies much deeper than in the fact that the Royal Arch stands at the head or summit of the Craft. It has two references to the capitular rank and consciousness of the Arch Mason himself. In virtue of his headship or supremacy over his material nature, he has passed beyond mere Craftwork and governed the Lodge of his lower nature, which he has now made the docile instrument and servant of his spiritual self. Henceforth, his energies are employed primarily on the spiritual plane. The "head" of the material organism of man is the spirit of man, and this spirit, consciously conjoined with the Universal Spirit, is Deity's supreme instrument and vehicle in the temporal world. Such a man's physical organism and brain have become sublimated and keyed up to a condition and an efficiency immensely in advance of average humanity. Physiological processes are involved, which cannot be discussed here beyond saying that in such a man, the entire nervous system contributes to charge certain ganglia and light up specific brain centers in a way that the ordinary mind knows nothing. The nervous system provides the storage batteries and conductive medium of the Spirit's energies, just as telegraph wires are the media for transmitting electrical energy. But the true Master Mason, in virtue of his mastership, knows how to control and apply those energies. They culminate and come to self-consciousness in his head, in his intelligence.

In this respect, we may refer to a very heavily veiled Theological testimony, the import of which goes quite unperceived by the inexperienced reader. The Gospels record that the Passion of the Great Exemplar and Master concluded "at the place called Golgotha in the Hebrew tongue; that is, the place of a skull." That is to say, it terminated in the head or seat of intelligence, and in a mystery of spiritual consciousness. The same truth is also testified to, though again under veils of symbolic phrasing, about the sprig of acacia planted at the head of the grave of the Masonic Grand Master and prototype, Hiram Abiff. The grave is the candidate's soul; the sprig of acacia typifies the latent *akasa* (to use an Eastern term) or divine germ planted in that soil and waiting to become quickened into activity in his intelligence, the "head" of that plane. When that sprig of acacia blooms at the head of his soul's tomb, he will understand at the same moment the mystery of Golgotha, the mystery of the death of Hiram, and the meaning of the Royal Arch ceremony of exaltation. It is a mystery of spiritual consciousness, the efflorescence of the mind in God, and the opening up of human intelligence in conscious association with the Universal and Omniscient Mind. This is why the cranium or skull is given prominence in the Master Mason's Degree.

With this introduced, we proceed to consider the Ceremony of Exaltation.

The Ceremony of Exaltation

Again, the candidate is in a state of darkness. However, the reason for this darkness differs entirely from that which existed at the stage of the Entered Apprentice. Then, he was an ignorant beginner upon the quest, making his first irregular unenlightened efforts towards the light. Now, he has long passed beyond that stage; he comes with all the qualifications and equipment of a Master Mason. Long ago, he found the light he first sought, and for a long time, he has been directing his steps and nourishing his growth with its rays. And more, after all this intimacy with it, he had known it receded from him and disappeared in the great ordeal of dereliction of the Third

Degree. It was there, in the "dark night of the soul" and utter helplessness of all his powers, he learned how strength could be perfected out of weakness by the potent efficacy of the Vital and Immortal Principle within him, in whose presence the darkness and the light are both alike. His present initial deprivation of light is the darkness of the Third Degree carried over into this further experience. It betokens rather a momentary failure to adjust his perception to the new quality of life he is now entering, just as a newborn child is unable at first to coordinate its sight to objects before it. For a while, but only briefly, the candidate feels himself in darkness but is blinded by an excess of light rather than by lack of it.

In this condition, he undertakes the opening out of a certain place, which he enters and explores, keeping in touch with his companions by a cord or lifeline. The symbolism of all this is singularly rich in allusion to certain interior processes of introspection well defined in the experience of the contemplative mystics and well attested in their records. The place entered emblematizes once again the material and psychical organism, a dense compact of material particles coating the more tenuous interior spirit of man as a shell surrounds the contents of an egg. "Roll away the stone," it will be recalled, was the first injunction of the Master at the raising of Lazarus. With this obstruction removed, the psychical organism becomes detached from the physical. The mind is free to become introverted and work exploratively upon its ground. It can search the contents of its unplumbed depths, to probe deeper and deeper into itself, eradicating defects and removing rubble, pushing in and in by the energy of a persistent will. Yet the mind can retain contact with the outer physical nature by a subtle filament or lifeline which prevents their entire separation. The position is the same as when the body sleeps while the mind is dreaming and vividly active. In dreams, the will does not function as a consciously directive instrument, as is hypothetically the case with one who, having attained mastership, has all his faculties under desire and control. Yet all this interior work, so rapidly summarized and symbolically enacted in the Ceremony, is not the work of a day nor the casual task of a weakling. The ancients referred to it as the twelve labors of Hercules, while its arduousness is further graphically described by the initiate poet Virgil in the sixth Æneid and by more recent illuminates. Nor, even when its nature is fully apprehended, is it a work to be lightly undertaken. Throughout the Ceremony, the utmost humility is enjoined upon the candidate as the essential qualification for entering this process of self-exploration. He is bidden to draw nigh to the Center but to halt and make obeisance at three several stages, at each of which he is told he is approaching more nearly to that central essence, that holy ground of his being upon which only the humble can walk, that "earth" which only the meek shall inherit.

In this state, the introverted mind, groping for its foundation and center, reaches at length the bedrock of its being. As the symbolic ceremony exhibits the grasping of an emblem embodying the Word of Life, so literally and the questing mind, in coming upon the Vital and Immortal Principle animating it, "lays hold on Eternal Life." It discovers the Lost Word, the divine root of its being, from which it has hitherto been so long dissociated. At first, it fails to realize the fact, for "the Light shineth in darkness and the darkness comprehendeth it not." Presently, that darkness will disappear when "the day (the new consciousness) dawns, and the shadows (the old mentality) flee away."

Therefore, this work of the introverted mind and its discovery are exhibited darkly and amid subterranean gloom. There remains, therefore, one concluding psychological process — to extrovert that knowledge and bring it forward into formalized brain consciousness so that what the spirit and the soul already know interiorly, the outer mind may also know exteriorly. Subjective awareness does not become knowledge until it has been recognized and passed through the alembic of the brain and logical understanding. When it has passed through and become formalized, a reciprocal and reflex action between the inner and outer natures is set up, illuminating the whole. This extroversion of subjective perceptions is symbolically achieved by the candidate's return from the subterranean depths to the surface, rejoining his former companion-sojourners and unifying all his component parts.

It is then that the Mystery is consummated—the Great Light breaks. The Vital and Immortal Principle comes to self-consciousness in him. The Glory of the Lord is revealed to and in him, and all his flesh sees it.

So far as symbolic ceremonial can *portceremoniess consummate* is represented by the restoration to light and the revelation that meets the candidate's gaze. His condition differs now from any that has preceded it. It is not merely illumination by Supernal Light. It is one of identification *with* It. He and It have become one, as a white-hot iron is indistinguishable from the furnace flame engulfing it. At the outset of his Masonic quest, the predominant wish of his heart was Light. The impulse was not his own; it was that of the Light Itself—the primal Light of Light, the Divine Word — seeking self-development in him. Consciousness is when light becomes self-perceptive by polarization within an efficient physiological organism. Man provides the only organism adapted to attaining that self-perception, but only when that organism is purified and prepared sufficiently for the achievement. In the Royal Arch, that achievement is hypothetically affected.

The condition attained by the illumined candidate is the equivalent of what in Christian theology is known as *Beatific Vision* and in the East as *Samadhi*. It is also considered universal or cosmic consciousness since the percipient transcends all sense of personal individualization, time, and space and is co-conscious with all that is. He has entered the bliss and peace surpassing that temporal understanding limited to perceiving the discords, antinomies, and contrasts characterizing finite existence; he has risen to that exalted state where all these find their resolution in the blissful concord of the Eternal. He is conscious of sympathy and has an identity of feeling with all that lives. He feels in virtue of that universal charity and limitless love which is the result of perceiving the unity of all in the Being of Deity. Which, at the outset of his progress, he was told was the summit of the Mason's profession. He also sees that there is a universe within and without him. He himself microcosmically sums up and contains all that manifested to his temporal intelligence as the vast universe around him. He is conscious of being the measure of the universe. He realizes that the earth, the heavens, and all their contents are externalizations, projected images, of corresponding realities present within himself. As the perfected head of creation, he beholds how he sums up all the lower forms of life through which his organism has passed to attain that perfection. The four symbolic standards exhibiting the lion, ox, man, and eagle are a very ancient glyph. They declare, among other things, the story of the soul's evolution and its progress from the passionate wild-beast stage to one which, while still sensuous and animal, is docile and disciplined for service. Then to the stage of human rationality, which at length culminates in upward-soaring spirituality. Similarly, the banners of the twelve tribes of Israel are figures of their prototypes, the twelve zodiacal sections of those heavens. Gathered beneath these emblems, are those who represent the tribes of no terrestrial nation, but are the "tribes of God." The heavenly hierarchies constitute an archetypal canopy or Holy Royal Arch above the visible creation and mediate to it the effluences of that all-embracing triune Spirit of Power, Wisdom and Love in which the entire composite structure lives, moves and has its being.

"In the beginning, God created the heavens and the earth, and the earth was without form and void, and darkness was upon the face of the deep. And God said, Let there be Light, and there was Light." With these words begins the Sacred Script, which is the sacramental token of that Living Word by whom all things were made, and are still in the making, and whose life is the light of men. The candidate who recovers that Lost Word, in the sense of regaining vital organic integration into it, and who, therefore, is one with its Life and its Light, can verify this old creation story in its application to himself. He stands in the presence of his own "earth" — the stone vault or dense matrix out of which his finer being has emerged — and of his own "heavens" or ethereal body of substantialized radiance which (as the iridescent sash of the Order is meant to denote) now covers him with light as with a garment. He can discern that he was first "without form and void" and who, in virtue of that *Fiat Lux* has at last become transformed from chaos and unconsciousness into a form so perfect and lucid as to become a co-conscious vehicle of Divine Wisdom itself.

With this symbolic attainment of Heavenly Vision and the restoration to Light, the effective part of the Royal Arch Ceremony as an initiatory rite concludes. An anti-climax and allegorical exposition follow, similar to the traditional history in the Master Mason's Degree. This takes the form of a mythos or dramatic narrative by the three sojourners, describing their release from captivity in Babylon. They returned to Jerusalem under an impulse to assist in rebuilding the destroyed national temple. The insightful mind will not fail to perceive in this historical or quasi-historical narrative an allegory of the spiritual process which has been going on within the candidate himself. He, as it is every human soul, has been in Babylonian bondage, in captivity to the Babel-confusion of mundane existence, the tyranny of material interests, and the chaos of his own disordered nature. He who is in revolt from these has in reflective moments "sat down and wept by the waters of Babylon" — the transient flux of temporal things. He "remembered Zion" in a yearning for inward freedom and permanent peace of heart. He finds the temple of his old natural self-worthless and in ruins and realizes that he must rebuild another and worthier one upon its site. From within himself comes the urge of the inward Lord (*Kurios*), which (under the mask of *Cyrus* the king) bids him forthwith to depart from his captivity and go up to his true native land and re-erect the Lord's house. He discovers plans and materials for the new structure among the rubble of his old self. And ultimately, when that new structure is completed and when from natural man, he has become reorganized into spiritual man. It is he who can perceive the wonders of his own constitution, to behold his own "earth" and his own "heavens" now fused into a unity to which both his material and his spiritual nature were necessary contributors.

The Chapter's constitution, as first revealed to the candidate, is, therefore, a symbol of his perfected organism. He sees that it is polarized East and West. The East is occupied by the three Principals, signifying his spiritual pole. The West, occupied by the three Sojourners, his psychic and materialized pole. Each triad being the reflex of the other, yet each triad being an organic unity in itself. St. John testifies to this (and the ceremonial rite is made conformable to the teaching of that great Initiate) when he writes: "There are three that bear record in heaven, and these three are one. And there are three that bear witness in earth, and these three agree in one." The meaning of this metaphysical assertion is that although monadic, essentially, is prismatically dissociable into a trinity. The Spirit in man in its triple aspects is, therefore, appropriately typified by the three Principals. They represent the three high attributes of the Spirit—Holiness, Royal Supremacy, and Functional Power—referred to in the title of the Order: Holy-Royal-Arch. These three middle and neutral terms must be considered as differentiating themselves into passive and active or negative and positive aspects. However, all three act conjointly and as one (as is, in fact, the case with the three Principals of a Chapter). These three aspects of the monadic Spirit are personified as Haggai (passive) and Joshua (active). Zerubbabel is the middle term from which the other two issue and into which they merge. For the central Majesty, one of its aspects is silent and withdrawn, and the other is functionally active and compulsive.

So, too, with the triad of Sojourners at the other pole. They represent the unitary human ego or personality in threefold aspects. They are the incarnated antitype or physicalized reflex of man's archetypal unincarnated and overshadowing Spirit. Hence, they are designated Sojourners or wayfarers upon a plane of impermanence, in contrast with the enduring life of the deathless spirit whose projection upon this lower world they are. Psychologically, human personality is distributed into a passive, negative subconsciousness and an active, positive intelligence. They are linked by a central coordinating principle. The combined three constituting man's unitary individuality. My ego, with its central and directive power of will, is my principal sojourner. My subconsciousness, with its passive intuitional capacity; and my practical intelligence, with its active and connecting powers of thought and understanding, are my assistant sojourners. They are clothed in white and able to reflect and react to their correspondences in the eastern or spiritual pole of my being.

The nexus or connecting medium between man's spiritual and bodily poles is represented by a third triad that the Scribes impersonated. The more important of these scribes is attached to the East Pole and is its emissary towards the West. The other is associated with the Western Pole, and his activities are directed Eastwards. The doorkeeper is the point of contact with the world without. In one of their many significances, they typify the middle term between Spirit and Matter—the astral medium or psychic bridge, in which contact between them is possible.

The Royal Arch Ceremony exhibits in a most graphic manner the psychological *rationale* of the final stage of regeneration. To the literalist, unacquainted with the fact that surface appearances are always intended to be transposed into spiritual values. The quasi-historic characters are meant to be impersonations of philosophic facts or principles. Some difficulty may be felt on being asked to translate the historical authenticity of the ceremonial text into the spiritualized interpretation here offered. However, the education and enlightenment of the understanding is one of the deliberate intentions of Initiatory Rites. Until the mind can rise above material facts and habituate itself to functioning in the more accurate realm of ideas that materialize into facts, there is a slight chance of its profiting from Rites like those of Masonry. Such Rites are of wholly negligible value but for the spiritual force and vitalizing energy of their inherent ideas. It may, therefore, be both helpful and a corroboration of what has been said if we scrutinize the Hebrew names of a Chapter's officers. What they yield upon analysis will demonstrate that those officers mimic ideas rather than represent persons.

1. "*Zerubbabel, prince of the people.*" The name means "a sprouting forth from Babel or among the people." "Babel" and "people" are two forms of expression of the same idea, and the English word is almost identical to the Hebrew one. Society as a whole, at all times of the world's history, constitutes a Babel of confused aims and interests. But there are always individuals intellectually or spiritually in advance of the crowd, and whose ideas, teachings, or examples shoot ahead of it, and to such leaders, the name Zerubbabel would apply. However, this illustration does not express the deeper sense that the word must be construed, which is *personal* application. The individual is himself a mob, a chaos, a multitude of confused desires, thoughts, and passions until these are brought into discipline. But, present even amidst these and sprouting up from among them, the ordinary man is conscious of a higher and spiritual element in him. He may cultivate or disregard this element, but in his best moments flames up above his lower

disordered nature, convinces him of the errors of his ways, and entices him to live on that higher level. That loftier element is expressed by the word "Zerubbabel." It is the apex and focus point of his spirituality as distinguished from his ordinary carnal intelligence, the summit of all his faculties, the "prince" of his "people." Those same faculties or "people" are referred to in the word meaning "My people having obtained mercy" (or become regenerate), and in the text, "The people that sat in darkness have seen a great light."

2. "*Haggai the Prophet.*" As shown before, the spiritual principle differentiates between passive and active. "Haggai" represents the passive aspect and signifies the blissful and self-contemplative nature of the spirit. It is called "the prophet" because of the power of insight and omniscience characterizing that which transcends the sense of time and abides eternally. Because it projects into the lower intelligence intuitions, fore glimpses and intimations of a prophetic nature. The same word is derived from the Greek word "*hagios,*" holy.

3. "*Joshua, the son of Josedek, the high priest,*" personifies the active executive aspect of spirit. Joshua means the "divine savior," and Josedek means "divine righteousness." While the "high priest" connotes a mediatorial factor between man and Deity. Therefore, the title implies that the human spirit or divine principle in man functions intermediately between the Deity and man's lower nature to promote the latter's salvation and perfection. We have previously shown how the Master Mason must be his high priest and "walk upon" the checkered floor-work of his elementary nature by learning to trample upon it. Thus, the Three Principals form a unity figuring man's spiritual pole in its triple aspects. They represent the summit of his being as it lives on the plane of the Spirit—holy, royal, supreme—blissful because in a state of holiness or wholeness; royal because a son of the King of all; powerful because of its power to subdue, transmute and redeem all that is below its purity and perfection.

4 & 5. *Ezra* and *Nehemiah*. In the great Mystery-system of Egypt, which long preceded the Hebrew system, the regenerate candidate, who had achieved the highest possible measure of self-transmutation of his lower nature, was accorded the title of Osiris. It was the equivalent of attaining Christhood. The nature of the perfecting process and the rituals in connection are available to us and are recommended to the student who desires to know how arduous that process was, and the extremely high degree of regeneration. In Hebrew, the name Osiris was changed into Azarias (and sometimes Zeruiah) and still further corrupted into Esdras and Ezra, the name of the senior Scribe of the Royal Arch. To understand the significance of the two Scribes, Ezra and Nehemiah, it is necessary to recall that these two were leading men in the Biblical account of the return from Babylonian captivity. Transposing this historical narrative into its spiritual implication, Ezra and Nehemiah personify two distinct stages of the mystical progress made by the candidate who seeks to renounce the Babel of his lower nature. It is done by reorganizing himself and regaining his native spiritual home and condition. "Nehemiah" (whose place in the Chapter is in the South West) is a figure of a certain measure of that reorganization and return. Like his Biblical prototype, he symbolizes the candidate engaged in rebuilding the wall of Jerusalem and occupied in the great work of self-reconstruction, from which he will not be fooled into coming down by the appeals and blandishments of the outer world. "Ezra" (whose position is in the North East) indicates a much more advanced measure of progress from West to East. The discerning student who will peruse the Biblical books of Nehemiah and Ezra (including the Apocryphal books of Esdras) in this light, and with this key to their true purport, will not fail to profit by the instruction they will yield. Hence, too, they are called "scribes;" both of them are recorders of, and testifiers to, distinct but representative experiences encountered in the inner man at different stages of the "great

work" of self-integration and journeying from a Babylon condition to the spiritual Jerusalem.

Here, we bring to an end our examination of the true meaning and purpose of the Royal Arch Ceremony. Dealing as it does with a supreme human experience which none can fully appreciate without undergoing it, it is the greatest and most influential rite in Masonry. No one who studies it comprehendingly and in its sacramental significance will withhold admiration either for the profound knowledge and insight of the now unidentifiable mystic and initiate who conceived it or for the skill with which he compiled it and cast his knowledge into dramatic expression. The pity is that those who practice the rite make no effort to penetrate its meaning and are content with the unenlightened perfunctory performance of a ritual that is even exoterically singularly striking, beautiful, and suggestive. The slightest reflection upon it must suggest that Masonry here is dealing with the building work of no outward structure. But it might be dealing with the re-erection of the fallen, disordered temple of the human soul and that even assuming that it memorialized some long past historical events, those events can have no vital bearing upon the life, character or conduct of anyone today. It would not justify the existence of an elaborate secret Order to perpetuate them. Suppose those events and this rite symbolize something deeper and personal. Suppose the sacramental truths are perpetually valid and capable of present realization in those who ceremonially re-enact them. In that case, they call for fuller and more serious attention than is usually accorded. Moreover, the Royal Arch is the symbolic representation of a supreme experience attained and attainable only in sanctity. It follows that the Craft Degrees leading up to and qualifying it will take on a much deeper sense than they commonly receive. They must be regarded as solemn instructions in the requisite preparation for that regenerative condition. The Craft work is unfinished without the attainment indicated in the Royal Arch.

That attainment, in turn, is impossible without the discipline of the preliminary labors, the purification of mind and desire, and that crucifixion unto death of the self-will. These acts constitute the tests of merit qualifying one for entrance to that Jerusalem which has no geographical site and which is called the "City of Peace" because it implies conscious rest of the soul in God. For many, the suggestion that attaining such a condition is possible or thinkable while we are still here in the flesh may be surprising or even incredible. But such doubt is unwarranted, and the Masonic doctrine negates it. As has already been shown to the contrary, that doctrine postulates not the absence but the possession of the material organism as a necessary factor in advancing the evolution of the human spirit. This organism is the vessel in which our base metal has to be transmuted into gold. It is the fulcrum furnishing the resistance requisite for the spirit's energizing into unfoldment and self-consciousness. Physical death is, therefore, not an advancement of, but an interference with, the work of regeneration. "The night cometh when no man can work," the soul merely passes from labor to refreshment until recalled to labor once more at the task of self-conquest. It is symbolic of that necessary dying to self, which implies the voluntary decreasing assertiveness of our temporal nature to permit a corresponding spiritual ascendancy.

But suppose in the hands of its present exponents Masonry is now a dead letter rather than a living effectual Initiatory Rite capable of quickening the spirituality of its candidates. In that case, it remains for the earnest and perspicuous aspirant to the deeper realities and instructive economy of the science of self-gnosis and regeneration. For such these papers are written, they may both learn something of the original design of the Order and educate their imagination in the principles of that science. And to such, in conclusion, maybe commended that Temple-hymn of the Hebrew Initiates, which of all the Psalms of David refers with most pointed reference to the subject matter of the Holy Royal

Arch of Jerusalem and the personal attainment of the blessed and perfected condition which that title implies:

> "I was glad when they said unto me,
> let us go up into the house of the Lord;
> Our feet shall stand within thy gates, O Jerusalem.
> Jerusalem is built as a city that is compact together;
> Thither the tribes go up, the tribes of the Lord. . ..
> For there are set thrones of judgment,
> the thrones of the house of David.
> Pray for the peace of Jerusalem!
> They shall prosper that love it.
> Peace is within her walls and
> plenteousness within her palaces.
> For my brethren and companions sake I will say,
> Peace be within thee. (*Psalm CXXII.*)

Those few lines are sketched, and all that is implied in the symbolic spectacle that greets the eyes of the Royal Arch Mason at the supreme moment of his restoration to light. Exalted into and become identified with the supreme bliss, peace, and self-consciousness of the All-Pervasive and Omniscient Spirit, he sees how he has "gone up" out of the Babylon of his old complex and disordered nature and upon its ruins has built for himself an ethereal body of glory, a "house of the Lord." He sees how this ecstatic condition, and this newly made celestial body are the sublimated products of his former self and its temporal organism. He sees how each separate part and faculty of that old nature, or as it were, each of the astrological divisions of his microcosm, has contributed its purified essence to form a new organism. "A new heaven and a new earth" and how these essences, like twelve diversified tribes, have assembled convergently and finally coalesced and become fused into a unity or new whole, "a city that is compact together." And it is this "city" which mystically is called

"Jerusalem," within whose walls is the peace which passes understanding and whose palaces reveal to the enfranchised soul the unfailing plentifulness and richness of the unbreakable trinity of Wisdom and Love and Power from which man and the universe have issued and into which they are destined to return.

The antithesis of this "heavenly city" is the confused Babylon city of this world, of which it is written to all captives therein, "Come out of her, My people, that ye be not partakers of her sins and that ye receive not of her plagues!" (*Rev.* xviii. 4). And, in a word, the Royal Arch Ceremony sacramentally portrays the last phase of the mystical journey of the exiled soul from Babylon to Jerusalem as it escapes from its captivity to this lower world and, "passing the veils" of matter and form, breaks through the bondage of corruption into the world of the formless Spirit and realizes the glorious liberty of the children of God.

Chapter V.
Freemasonry in Relation to the Ancient Mysteries

EVERY Mason is naturally desirous of knowing something about the origin and history of the Craft. The available literature on the subject is verbose and unsatisfying. It offers many disconnected details of archeology and comparative religion without unifying them in any helpful light. It deals with matters of minor and temporal history rather than with what alone is of real moment, the spiritual lineage of the Craft. In this paper, therefore, it is proposed to trace a rough outline of a movement that is as old as humanity itself and the purpose and doctrine of which are still faithfully, if very rudimentarily, preserved in the Masonic system. But such an incomplete sketch may perhaps prove more serviceable than a mass of fragmentary facts over which one may pore indefinitely and with much interest, yet without perceiving their inter-relation or coordinating them into one comprehensive impressive scheme.

No effective work upon Masonry exists that treats its history and purpose in the only way that matters vitally. The student is apt to waste much time and little profit by turning to information in publications, the titles of which seem to promise full enlightenment, but that leaves him unsatisfied and unconvinced. Random collections of information on points of symbolism, archeology, and anthropology and tracing connections between modern Masonry and medieval building-guilds and other communities may all be very interesting. Still, these are as the dry bones of a subject of which one desires to know the living spirit. They fail to answer the main questions one asks from the heart and is anxious to have answered. Questions such as, what was the nature of the Ancient Mysteries that modern Masonry purports to perpetuate? To what end and purpose did they exist? What need is there to perpetuate them today? For what purpose was Initiation instituted? Did it serve any real purpose at any time, or can it now? Was it ever more than it is today, a mere perfunctory ceremonial leading to nothing of essential value and emphasizing only a few moral principles and elementary truths that we know already? The goal of this paper is to attempt to answer such questions.

Now, one of the first things to strike any student of Masonic literature and comparative religion is the remarkable presence of common factors, beliefs, doctrines, practices, and symbols in the various religions. These common traits exist whether ancient or modern, eastern or western, civilized or barbarian, Christian or pagan. However separated from others by time or distance, however intellectualized or primitive their religion or morals each people is found to have employed and still to be employing certain ideas, symbols, and practices in common with every other. Masonic treatises abound with proof of this uniformity in using various symbols prominent in every lodge. Authors delight in supplying evidence of the close correspondences in various unrelated systems and in demonstrating how ancient and universal such ideas, symbols, and practices have been. But they do not go so far as to explain the reason for this antiquity and universality. It is this point which will be well to clear up at the outset since it furnishes the clue to the entire problem of the genesis, the history, and the reason for the existence of Masonry.

Suppose research and reflection are pushed far enough. In that case, it becomes clear that the universality and uniformity referred to are because, at one time, long back in the world's past, there existed or was implanted in the minds of the whole human family—which was doubtless much smaller and more concentrated then than now—a Proto-Evangelium or Root-Doctrine regarding the nature and destiny of the soul of man and its relation to the Deity. Today we pride ourselves upon being wiser and more advanced than primitive humanity.

We assume that our ancestors lived in moral darkness, and we have since gradually emerged into comparative light. All the evidence, however, rebuffs these suppositions. It indicates that primitive man, however childish or intellectually undeveloped according to modern standards, was spiritually conscious and psychically perceptive to a degree undreamed of by the modern mind. It is us who, for all our cleverness and intellectual development in temporal matters, are nevertheless plunged in darkness and ignorance about our nature, the invisible world around us, and the eternal spiritual realities. In all Scriptures, the tradition is universal of a "Golden Age." An age of comparative innocence, wisdom, and spirituality, in which racial unity and individual happiness through enlightenment prevailed. It is one in which there was that open vision for want of which a people perished, but in virtue of which men were once in conscious conversation with the unseen world. They were shepherded, taught and guided by the "gods" or discarnate superintendents of the infant race, who imparted to them the sure and indefeasible principles upon which their spiritual welfare and evolution depended.

The tradition is also universal of the collective soul of the human race having sustained a "fall," a moral declension from its true path of life and evolution. This fall has severed it almost entirely from its creative source. As the ages advanced, it has involved its sinking more and more deeply into physical conditions. It is splitting up from a unity employing a single language into a diversity of conflicting races of different speeches and degrees of moral advancement. It is accompanied by progressive densification of the material body and a corresponding darkening of the mind and atrophy of the spiritual consciousness. The statement to some who read this will probably be rejected as fabulous and incredible. The supposition of a "fall of man" is nowadays an unpopular doctrine, rejected by many who contend that everything points instead to a rise of man. Yet, who fails to reflect that logically, a rise necessarily involves an antecedent fall from which a rise becomes possible. We cannot stop discussing this point. We must be content merely by indicating what is unanimously recorded as fact in both the Scriptures of all races and the Wisdom-tradition of the sages of antiquity.

From that "fall," which was not due to the transgression of an individual but to some weakness or defect in the collective or group soul of the Adamic race (humanity). This "fall" was not a matter of a moment but a process covering vast time cycles. It was necessary and within the Divine counsels and providence that humanity should be redeemed and restored to its pristine state. It should be brought back once more into vital association with the Divine Principle from which by its secession it became increasingly detached, as its materialistic tendencies overpowered and vast time cycles for its achievement. And it needed something further. It required the application of an orderly and scientific method to affect the restoration of each fallen soul fragment and bring it back to its primitive, pure, and perfect condition. I emphasize that the process was necessarily not haphazard but scientific. Anyone may fall from a housetop and break his bones; skilled surgery and intelligent effort are required to heal the patient and get him back to the place prior to the fall. So, with humanity. The fall was out of Eden, as our Scriptures describe — why and how, again, we must not stay to enquire. The fall was through inherent weakness and lack of wisdom. Unable to affect its recovery, it required skilled scientific assistance from other sources to restore it. Whence could come that skill and scientific knowledge if not from the Divine and now invisible world? Would not that regenerative method be properly described if it were called, as in Masonry it *is* called, a "heavenly science," and welcomed in the words that Masons use, "Hail, Royal Art!"?

Thus, then, was the origin and birth of Religion. Religion is a word that implies a "binding back" (*re-ligare*). As with the setting and bandaging of a broken limb, so the collective soul of humanity needed to be restored to the condition from which it had become dislocated and once more built into a perfectly harmonious whole.

To the spiritual guardians of primitive man, one must attribute the communication of that universal science of rebuilding the fallen temple of humanity. In this science, we are now surprised to find traces of this in every race and religion. To this source, we must credit the distribution, in every land and among every people, of the same or equivalent symbols, practices, and doctrines, modified only locally and by the intelligence of peoples, yet all manifesting a common root and purpose.

This was the one holy catholic (the word "catholic" meaning "universal") religion "throughout all the world," at once, it was a theoretical doctrine and a practical science intended to reunite man with his Maker. That religion could only be one, as, if not, it could not be catholicism and for all men equally and alike. However, owing to the perverse distortive tendencies of humanity itself, it was susceptible to becoming (as has so happened) debased and sectarianized into as many forms as there are peoples. Moreover, its main principles could never be susceptible to alteration. However, they might be (as they have been) exoterically understood by some and esoterically by others, and their full import would only sometimes be apparent but develop with increasing fidelity to and understanding of them. It provided the unalterable "landmarks" of knowledge concerning human nature, human potentialities, and human destiny. It laid down the ancient and established "usages and customs" to always be followed by everyone content to accept its discipline, which none might deviate from or add innovations to, save at his own peril. It was the "Sacred Law" for the guidance of the fallen soul, a law valid from the dawn of time till its sunset, and of which it is written, "As it was in the beginning, is now and ever shall be, world without end." It was the science of life—of temporal limited life lived with the intention of its conversion and sublimation into eternal universal life. Therefore, it called for a scientific or philosophical method of living, every moment and action of which should be directed to that great goal. This is a very different method from the modern method, which is entirely practical in its outlook and unscientific in its conduct.

This Proto-Religion is related to having originated in the East, from which proverbially all Light comes. As humanity itself became diffused and distributed over the globe, it gradually spread towards the West, in a perpetual watchfulness of humanity's spiritual interests and an unfailing purpose to retrieve "that which was lost" — the fallen human soul. We have already said that in early times, humanity then, under its influence, was far less materialized and far more spiritually sensitive and perceptive than it subsequently became, or is now. Accordingly, it follows that with the increasing age and density of the race, the influence of the Proto-Religion itself became correspondingly diminished. However, its principles remained as valid and effectual as before, for man's self-willed impulses and speculative conceptions cannot alter the principles of static Truth and Wisdom. To follow in any detail the course of its history is not now necessary and would require a lengthy treatise. To do so would also be like following the course of a river backward from its broad mouth to a point where it becomes an insignificant and scarcely traceable channel. The race has wandered backward, farther from the original Wisdom-teaching so that the once broad and bright flood of Light upon cosmic principles and the evolution of the human soul has now become contracted into minute points. But that Light, like that of a Master Mason, has never been wholly extinguished, however dark the age, and, by the tradition, this of ours is spiritually the darkest of the dark ages. "God has never left Himself without a witness among the children of men." Among the witnesses to the Ancient Wisdom and Mysteries is the system of Masonry; a faint and feeble flicker, perhaps, but nevertheless a true Light and in the actual line of succession of the primitive doctrine, and one still able to guide our feet into the way of peace and perfection.

The earliest teaching of the Mysteries traceable within historical time was in the Orient and in the Sanscrit language — a significant and appropriate name, for it means Holy Writ or *"Sanctum Scriptum."* For very great Lights upon the ancient Secret Doctrine, one must still refer to India's religious and philosophical scriptures, which were in their spiritual and temporal prime when modern Europe was frozen beneath an ice cap.

But societies, like men, have their infancy, manhood, and old age. They are but units, upon a larger scale than the individual, for furthering the general life purpose. When a given society has served or failed in that purpose, the stewardship of the Mysteries passes on to other and more productive hands. The next great torch-bearer of the Light of the World was Egypt, which, after many centuries of spiritual supremacy, in turn, became the arid desert it now is both spiritually and materially. It left, nevertheless, a mass of structural and written relics still testifying to its possession of the Doctrine in the days of its glory. From Egypt, as civilizations developed in adjoining countries, a great irradiation of them took place by the diffusion of its knowledge and the institution of minor centers for imparting the Divine Science in Chaldea, Persia, Greece, and Asia Minor. "Out of Egypt have I called My son" is, in one of its many senses, a biblical allusion to this passing on of the catholic Mysteries from Egypt to new regions for their enlightenment.

Of these various translations, those that concern us chiefly are two: the one to Greece, the other to Palestine. We know from the Bible that Moses was an initiate of the Egyptian mysteries and became learned in all its wisdom. At the same time, Philo tells us that Moses there became "skilled in music, geometry, arithmetic, hieroglyphics, and the whole circle of arts and sciences." In other words, he became, in a real sense, a Master Mason and, as such, qualified himself for his subsequent great task of leadership of the Hebrew people and the formulating of their religious system and rule of life as laid down in the Pentateuch. The Mosaic system continued, as we know, along the channel indicated in the books of the Old Testament, and then, after many centuries and deviations, crystallized in the greatest of all expressions of the Mysteries, as disclosed in the Gospels of the New Testament (or New Witness), involving the supersession of all previous systems under the Supreme Grand Mastership of Him who is called the Light of the World and its Savior.

Concurrently with the existence of the Hebrew Mysteries under the Mosaic dispensation, the great Greek school of the Mysteries was developing, which, originating in the Orphic religion, culminated and came to a focus at Delphi and generated the philosophical wisdom and the esthetic glories associated with Athens and the Periclean age. Greece was the spiritual descendant and infant prodigy of India and Egypt, though developing along quite different lines. We know that Pythagoras, like Moses, after absorbing all his native teachers could impart, journeyed to Egypt to take his final initiation before returning and founding the great school at Crotona associated with his name. We know, too, from the *Timæus* of Plato how aspirants for mystical wisdom visited Egypt for initiation and were told by the priests of Sais that "you Greeks are but children" in the Secret Doctrine but were admitted to information enabling them to promote their spiritual advancement. We know from the correspondence, recorded by Iamblichus, between Anebo and Porphyry of the fraternal relations existing between the various schools or lodges of instruction in different lands. Their members visited, greeted, and assisted one another in the secret science, the more advanced being obliged, as every initiate still is when called upon, to "afford assistance and instruction to his brethren in the inferior degrees." And we know that at the Nativity — or shall we say the installation in this world — of the Great Master, there came to Him from afar Magi or initiate-visitors who knew of His impending advent and had seen His Star in the East and desired to acknowledge and pay Him reverence. In all these world-moving incidents in times when initiation was an actual event and not a mere ceremonial form as now, it is of interest to notice the practice upon a grand scale of the same customs and courtesies as are still observed, though alas unintelligently, by the Craft of today.

We must now speak more fully of the Mysteries and the "Royal Art" as pursued by the Greek school. With the Greeks, it took the form of a quest of philosophy, *i.e.*, for wisdom, for the Sophia, just as in the Hebrew and Christian schools, it took the form of a quest for the Lost Word. The end was, of course, the same in both cases, but the approach to it was by different means, and, as we shall see, the two methods later merged into one. The Greek approach was primarily an intellectual one and by what Spinoza has termed *Amor intellectualis Dei*. The Christian approach was primarily through the affections and the heart's adoration. Both strained after "that which was lost," but one sought after the lost ideal intellectually and the other through devotional energy. Humanity is slowly educated, "line upon line; precept upon precept; here a little and there a little," one faculty after another being developed and trained to refashion the perfect organism. And if philosophical Wisdom and the sense of Beauty stood forth — as they did stand forth — then it was most prominently as the main pillars of the Greek system. The Greeks had yet to learn of a third and middle pillar that synthesized and comprised them both — that of the Strength of the supreme virtue of Love, when towards the object of all desire it pours from a pure and perfect heart.

The Greek quest for wisdom was more than a desire for more information and mature judgment about one's place in the universe. Merely knowing facts about the hidden side of life profits nothing unless the knowledge is allowed to influence and adapt our method of living to the truths disclosed. Then, knowledge becomes transmuted into wisdom; one becomes the truth one sees, and a man's life becomes a substantial and dynamic truth. But to bring this about, one must first be informed about or initiated into certain elements of the truth and be persuaded that it is true before setting about becoming it. The Greek method, therefore, began by initiating the mind into certain truths about the soul's nature, history, destiny, and potentialities. It then left the individual to follow up the information by a course of conduct in which the teaching imparted would become converted into assured conviction and living power. At the same time, his increasing scientific progress would awaken him to still deeper truths.

It cannot be overemphasized that no one can learn spiritual science, whether as taught by Masonry or any other system inculcating it, without submitting himself to its processes and living them out in practical experience. In this supreme study, knowing depends entirely upon doing; comprehension is conditional upon and the result of action. "He that will *do*, the will shall *know* of the doctrine."

Hence, in Masonry, an installed Master is still called a "*Master* of Arts and Sciences," for he is supposed to have mastered the art of living by the theoretic gnosis or science imparted to him during his progress. Real Masonic knowledge will never be achieved merely by oral explanation, hearing lectures, and studying books. These may be useful in giving a preliminary start to earnest seekers needing a little guidance for setting them on that path of personal practice and experience. But they will soon develop an automatic understanding of the doctrine for themselves. Those with but a casual interest in the doctrine will continue to find what is of true value to be veiled and secret. For example, it is one thing to hear explained what is meant by being divested of money and metals in the philosophical sense. It is quite another thing to have become insusceptible to all attraction by material interests and sense-allurements and to be consciously possessed of the wisdom accruing from that experience. It may be interesting to be told why, at a particular stage of progress, the candidate is likened to an ear of corn by a fall of water. Still, the explanation may be forgotten tomorrow. For as the result of his effort, the hearer has become personally aware of a substantial growth ripening to harvest within him from the ground of his being and fertilized by supersensual nourishment falling like the gentle rain from Heaven upon his ardent and aspiring soul. Again, it may seem instructive to know that the great ritual of the Third Degree signifies a death unto sin and self and a new birth unto righteousness. But how will the information profit those who nevertheless mean to go on living the old manner of life, which at every moment negates all that that ritual implies?

The Ancient Mysteries involved much more than merely abstract philosophy. They also required a philosophical method of living — or instead of dying. For as Socrates said (in Plato's *Phædo*, from which much Masonic teaching is directly drawn and which every Masonic student should study deeply), "the whole study of the philosopher (or wisdom-seeker) is nothing else than to die and be dead." It is an assertion repeated by Plutarch, "to be initiated is to die"; and by the Christian apostle, "I die daily." Their method was divided into the Lesser and the Greater Mysteries. The Lesser were those in which the more elementary instruction was imparted so that candidates might immediately purify and adapt their lives to the truths disclosed. The Greater Mysteries were related to the developments of consciousness within the soul itself. To draw a faint analogy, the Lesser Mysteries bore the same relation to the Greater as the present Craft Degrees to the Holy Royal Arch.

Dealing adequately with the mystery systems would involve a lengthy study. We will refer to one of the most famous of them, the Eleusinian, which existed in Greece and was the focus point of religion and philosophy for the then-civilized portion of Europe for several centuries. "Eleusis" means Light, and initiation into the Mysteries of Eleusis, therefore, meant a quest of the aspirant for Light, in precisely the same, but a far more accurate, sense as the modern Mason declares Light to be the predominant wish of his heart. It meant not merely light in the sense of being given some secret information not obtainable elsewhere or about any matter of worldly interest but the opening up of the candidate's whole intellectual and spiritual nature in the supersensual Light of the Divine world and raising him to God-consciousness. The ordinary and uninitiated man knows nothing of that supersensual Light by merely his natural reason. He is conscious only of the outer world and things perceptible by his natural faculties. In the words of St. Paul, "The natural man receiveth not the things of the Spirit of God, for they are foolishness unto him; neither can he know them because they are spiritually discerned." Initiation meant a process whereby natural man became transformed into a spiritual or ultra-natural man. It was necessary to *change his consciousness*, to gear it to a new and higher principle, and so, as it were, make of him a new man in the sense of attaining a new method of life and a new outlook upon the universe. "Be ye transformed by the renewing of your minds," says the Apostle, referring to this process. The transference of the symbol of the Divine Presence from the ceiling to the floor of the Masonic Lodge indicates how the Vital and Immortal Principle in man can be brought down from his remoter psychological region into his physical organism and function there through his body and brain, thus as it were dislocating and superseding his natural mentality and regenerating him. This truth is still further reproduced in Masonry by the name "Lewis," traditionally associated with the Craft. "Lewis" is a modern corruption of Eleusis and other Greek and Latin names associated with Light. In our instruction lectures, it is said that we should designate "the son of a Mason." This, however, has no reference to human parentage. It refers to the mystical birth of the Divine Light in oneself. A familiar Scriptural text states, "Unto us, a child is born, unto us a son is given." It is the Divine Principle, the Divine Wisdom, brought to birth and function within the organism of the natural man, who virtually becomes its parent. It is further described in our lectures as something "which, when properly dovetailed into a stone, forms a clamp, enabling Masons to lift great weights with little inconvenience while fixing them on their proper bases." All of which is a concealed way of expressing the fact that when the Divine Light is brought forward from man's submerged depths and firmly grafted or dovetailed into his natural organism. He then becomes able to grapple easily with difficulties, problems, and "weights" of all kinds.

When the Mysteries flourished, every educated man entered them the same way men entered a university in modern times. They were the recognized source of instruction in the only things that matter, those affecting the culture of the human soul and its education in the science of itself and its divine nature. Candidates were graded according to their moral efficiency and intellectual or spiritual stature. For years, they underwent disciplinary intellectual exercises and bodily self-control, punctuated at intervals by appropriate tests and ordeals to determine their fitness to proceed to the more serious, solemn, and awful processes of actual initiation, administered only to the duly qualified, and which were of a secret and closely guarded character. Their education, differing greatly from the scholastic methods of a utilitarian age like our own, was directed solely to the cultivation of the "four cardinal virtues" and the "seven liberal arts and sciences" as qualifications prerequisite to participation in the higher order of life to which initiation would eventually admit the worthy and properly prepared candidate. The construction of these virtues and sciences was much more advanced than the modern mind considers adequate. Virtues with them were more than abstractions and ethical sentiments; as the word implies, they involved positive strength and courage of the soul. Temperance involves complete control of the passional nature under every circumstance; Fortitude, the courage that no adversity will dismay or deflect from the goal in view; Prudence, the deep insight that begets the prophetic or forward-seeing faculty of seer-ship (*providentia*); Justice unswerving righteousness of thought and action. The "arts and sciences" were called "liberal" because they tended to liberate the soul from defects and illusions normally enslaving it. This is totally differing from science in the modern sense, the tendency of which is, as we know, materialistic and soul-benumbing. Grammar, Logic, and Rhetoric with the Ancients were disciplines of a moral nature by which the irrational tendencies of a human being were purged away. He was trained to become a living witness of the universal Logos and a living mouthpiece of the Divine Word. Geometry and Arithmetic were sciences of transcendental space and numeration (seeing that, as in the words of our Scriptures, God has "made everything by measure, number and weight"). Comprehension of what was taught provides the key, not only to the problems of one's being but to those physical ones which are found so baffling by the inductive methods of today. Astronomy required no telescopes. It dealt not with the stars of the sky but was the science of metaphysics and understanding the distribution of the forces latent in and determining the destiny of individuals and their nations. Finally, Music (or Harmony) was for them not of the vocal or instrumental kind. It meant the living practice of philosophy, the adjustment of human life into harmony with God until the personal soul became unified with Him and consciously heard because it now participated in, the music of the spheres. As Milton puts it:

"How lovely is Divine Philosophy,
  Not harsh and crabbèd as dull fools suppose,
  But musical as is Apollo's lute
  And a perpetual feast of nectar'd sweets
  Where no crude surfeit reigns."

Every possible device was employed and practiced training the mind to acquire dominion over the passions and to loosen and detach it from the impressions and attractions of the senses. The goal was to destroy the illusions and false imaginations under which it labors when using no higher light than its own, and to qualify it for a higher method of cognition and the reception of supersensual truth and the light of the Divine world. The idealism of Greek architecture and sculpture was entirely due to the same motive: to elevate the imagination beyond the visible level and fit the mind for the apprehension of ultra-physical form and beauty. Even athletic exercises were made to subserve the same purpose. Wrestling and racing were not simple sports, they were regarded sacramentally. They were seen as the type of combats the soul must engage in against the fleshly desires and the victor's crown of laurel or olive was the emblem of wisdom and illumination resulting to him in whom the spirit conquers the flesh. Thus, every intellectual and physical interest was made subservient to the one idea of separating the soul from material bondage. It was purposely of a purifying or "cathartic" nature that should cleanse the thoughts and desires of the aspirant. All was to make him "white" within and without, even as the modern candidate for the Craft is clothed in white. This inward purity of heart and mind, coupled with the possession of the four cardinal virtues, was and still is essential to the ordeals of actual initiation. Those who became proficient and properly prepared in this curriculum of the Lesser Mysteries were eventually admitted to initiation in the Greater Mysteries. Those who failed to qualify were restrained from advancement. The numbers of earnest and qualified aspirants were only a percentage of those who entered the Mysteries. For in spiritual life, as in the world of nature, the biological phenomenon prevails that the available raw material greatly exceeds the perfected product. Every year, far more seeds are borne, and far more eggs are laid or spawned than reach maturity, although every seed and egg can grow and fruition. Plato, speaking of the Mysteries in his day, quotes a still older authority that "the thyrsus-bearers (or candidates for initiation) are numerous, but the *Bacchuses* (or perfected initiates) are few." The same truth is restated in the words in the Gospels, "Many are called, but few are chosen."

One qualification above all was essential to the aspirant, as it still is today—humility. The wisdom into which the Mysteries and initiation admit a man is a foolishness to the world. It is a reversal and revolution of all orthodox and academic standards. To attain it, a man must be prepared for that complete and voluntary self-denial, which may involve his finding negating everything he has previously held to be true or which those among whom he ordinarily mingles believe to be true. He must be content to "become a fool for the kingdom of heaven's sake" and suffer adversity, ridicule, and blame if needed. This was one of the prime reasons for secrecy and one—though not the only one—of the origins of the Masonic injunction to secrecy. The world's wisdom and that to which initiation admits are so antipodal that any intrusion of the latter will infallibly provoke resentment from the former. Hence, it is written, "Cast not your pearls before swine, neither give that which is holy unto dogs—*lest they turn and rend you.*" Therefore, silence and secrecy are desirable if only in self-defense, though there are other reasons; humility is indispensable. In the public processions of the Lesser Mysteries—for the public was permitted at certain festivals to participate to a small extent in some of the more exoteric knowledge—the sacred emblems and eucharistic vessels used in the rites were carried with great reverence upon the back of an ass. With the same intention, it is said that one of the great Greek philosophers always had an ass by his side in his lecture-room when instructing his students. The explanation is given in the words of one of the old authorities upon initiation as follows: "There is no creature so able to receive divinity as an ass, into whom if ye be not turned, ye shall in no wise be able to carry the divine mysteries." In the light of this, one will at once discern the symbolical significance of the Christian Master riding into Jerusalem upon an ass.

Another considerably educative means employed in the Mysteries was instructing, enlarging, and purifying the imagination through myths, expressing either in doctrinal form or by spectacular representation, truths of the Divine world and the soul's history. The modern mind, in its passion for actual concrete facts, has little sympathy for a method of teaching that dispenses with demonstrable facts. However, facts—of history or science—tend to congest the mind and paralyze the imagination, as Darwin lamented in his case. Principles stimulate and illumine the imagination and enable the mind to interpret facts and adjust them to their proper relation. The Greek mythologists were adept at expressing universal and philosophical truths in the guise of fables. By design, these fables were addictively interesting and yet expressed theosophical teachings to the discerning and veiled it from the careless and ignorant. Myth-making was a science, not an indulgence in irresponsible fiction, and by exhibiting some of these myths in dramatic form, candidates were instructed in various fundamental principles of life.

One of the chief and best-known of the numerous myths was that of Demeter and her daughter Persephone. This myth is annually performed with great ceremony and elaboration at the Greek festival, Eleusinia, and of which it may be useful to speak briefly. It told how the maiden Persephone strayed away from Arcadia (Heaven) and her mother, Demeter, to pluck flowers in the meadows. To her surprise, the soil opened and caused her to fall through into the lower dark world of Hades. The despair of her mother at the loss reached Zeus, the chief of the gods. Zeus took pity on Demeter and ordained that if the girl had not eaten of the fruit of Hades, she should immediately be restored to her mother forever. But if she had so eaten she must abide a third of each year in Hades and return to Demeter for the other two thirds. Persephone had unfortunately eaten a pomegranate in the lower world, so her restoration to her mother could not be permanent but only periodic.

This myth and the importance once attached to it will be appreciated only upon understanding its interpretation. It is the story of the soul and is of the same nature as the Mosaic myth of Adam and Eve and the apple. As also is the universal parable of the Prodigal Son. Neither of these stories is meant to be regarded as historically accurate. They are fictional accounts of spiritual cosmic facts. Persephone is the human soul, generated out of that primordial incorruptible mother-earth which the Greeks personified as Demeter. Her straying from her Arcadian home and heavenly mother in quest for flowers (or fresh experiences) in the meadows of Enna correspond with the same promptings of desire that led to Adam's disobedience in Eden and his fall thence to this outer world. All willful desires end in dissatisfaction and bitterness, and "Enna" (signifying darkness and bitterness) is the same word that still meets us in Gehenna. One may, however, profit from one's mistakes. They breed wisdom, and the riches of wisdom and experience are signified by Pluto, the god of riches, into whose kingdom Persephone falls. She might have returned thence to her mother forever, Zeus decreed, had she not still further injured herself by eating the fruit of the lower world. But having done so, her restoration can only be partial and temporary. This alludes to the soul's further self-soilure and degradation by lusting after the inferior pleasures of this lower plane, which, as the pomegranate symbolizes, is many-seeded with illusions and vanities. Until these false tendencies are eradicated, until the desires of the heart are utterly weaned from external delights, there can be no permanent restoration of the soul to its source.

Through this great myth, instruction was imparted on the history of the soul, its destiny, and its prospects, and the doctrine of reincarnation **was emphasized**.

Now, Masonry follows this traditional method of instruction based on myths. Its canon of teaching in the Craft degrees contains two myths. One is that of the building of King Solomon's Temple. The other is the death and burial of Hiram Abiff, which is narrated in traditional history. The Royal Arch contains a third myth in the story of the return from captivity after the destruction of the first temple, the commencement of building the second, and the discovery then made. This third myth has already been expounded in our paper on the Royal Arch degree, so we need now speak only of the Craft Myths.

To the literal-minded, the building of Solomon's temple at Jerusalem (which is, of course, largely but not entirely based upon the Hebrew Scriptures) appears to be the history of an actual structure erected by three Asiatic notables, one of whom conceived the idea, another supplying the building material. At the same time, the third was the practical architect and chief of the works. The previous two are said to have been kings of adjacent small nations; the third was not royalty but a person of no social dignity and a "widow's son."

As has previously been said in these papers, these details of an enterprise undertaken more than two thousand years ago can have no possible value to anyone today. If they were related merely to historical facts, modern Masonry might as well close its doors and cease to exist for any benefit those facts could impart to serious or reflective minds. But the narrative might never have been intended as a record of historical facts but as a myth enshrining philosophic truths concerning eternal principles. It must be interpreted with spiritual discernment, and its analysis will reveal matters of fundamental importance.

The story of the temple building, then, is a philosophical instruction, garbed in quasi-historical form concerning the structure of the human soul. That temple is not one of common brick and stone but of the "unhewn stone" or incorruptible raw material of which the Creator fashioned the human organism. The Jerusalem in which it was built was not the geographical one but the eternal "city of peace" in the Heavens. As St. Paul says, "the Jerusalem above, which is the mother of us all." Its builders were not three human personages, but the Divine energy considered in its three constituent principles spoken of in our Instruction Lectures as Wisdom, Strength, and Beauty. These "pillars of His work" run through and form the metaphysical principles defined in modern terms as Life-Essence (or the substantial spirit of Wisdom). They are the incorruptible Matter, serving as the matrix or vehicle of that Life-Essence to give it fixity, form, and objectiveness (Strength). And lastly is the intellectual principle or Logos binding these together and constituting the whole as an intelligent and functionally effective instrument (Beauty). Of these three principles, or upon these three pillars, was the human soul originally and divinely built in the heaven-world. Our Lectures, therefore, rightly say that those three pillars "also allude to Solomon, King of Israel; Hiram, King of Tyre; and Hiram Abiff," because those names personify the indissociable triadic constituents of the Divine Unity. (They are also inscribed upon the central symbolic altar in the Royal Arch Degree as further evidence of this divine construction of the human soul).

However, the temple of the soul has now been destroyed and thrown down from its primitive eminence and grandeur. Instead of being a collective united organic whole, humanity has become shattered into innumerable fragmentary separated parts, not one stone standing upon another of its ruined building. It has lost consciousness of the genuine secrets of its origin and nature and is now content with the spurious substituted knowledge it picks up from sense impressions in this outer world. Like Persephone, it has eaten the pomegranates of Pluto's dark realm in preference to the ambrosia of Arcady. Until that poison is eliminated from its system, it cannot permanently reclaim its unfallen state. For now, it must, at best, endure a rhythm of deaths and rebirths and intermittent periods of labor in this world and refreshment beyond it.

A further word is necessary regarding the concealed significance of Solomon and the two Hirams. Solomon personifies the primordial Life-Essence or substantialized Divine Wisdom, which is the basis of our being. It is defined in the *Book of Wisdom* (chap. vii., 25-27) as "a pure influence flowing from the glory of the Almighty; the brightness of the everlasting light, the unspotted mirror of the power of God and the image of His goodness." It is described as a "king" because it needs to transcend and over-rule whatever is inferior to itself, and as "King of Israel" because "Israel" itself means "cooperating or ruling with God" as distinct from being associated with beings or affairs of a sub-divine order. To conjoin this transcendental Life-Essence to a vehicle, which should give it fixity and form, requires the assistance of another dominant or "kingly" principle, personified as Hiram, King of Tyre, who supplied the "building material." Since we are dealing with purely metaphysical ideas, it will be obvious that the Tyre in question has no relation to the Levantine seaport of that name. The name Tyre in Hebrew means "rock," and we associate the strength, compactness, and durability with rock. At the same time, the same word recurs in Greek as *Turos* and in Latin as *Terra*, earth, and *Durus*, implying form, hardness, consistency, and durability. "King of Tyre," therefore, is interpretable as the cosmic principle that gives solidity and form to the spiritual fluidic and formless Life-Essence, and which is comparable to a cup intended to hold liquid. Solomon and Hiram of Tyre, therefore, contribute their respective properties of Life-Essence and durable form and "building material" as the groundwork of the soul, which then is made functionally effective by the addition of the third principle described as Hiram Abiff, the widow's son, and personifying the active intellectual principle or Logos. In a word, Hiram Abiff is the Christ-principle immanent in every soul; crucified, dead, and buried in all who are not alive to its presence, but resident in all as a saving force—"Christ in you, the hope of glory." Consistently with Christ-like humility, Hiram Abiff (literally, "the teacher from the Father") is not described as a "king" as are Solomon and Hiram of Tyre, but as one "of no reputation," a "widow's son." This is a striking touch of Gnostic symbolism referable to the neglected or widowed nature of the Divine Motherhood or Sophia owing to the errancy and defection from wisdom of her frail children. Such children as have rejoined or are striving to rejoin, their mother is alone worthy of being called the "Widow's Sons." It is to the cry to those who have rejoined her from those still laboring at that task in the flesh. Perhaps wiping from their brow the bloody sweat of their Gethsemane anguish in the struggle, that the traditional petition applies, "Come to my help, ye sons of the Widow, for I am the Widow's son!"

The temple of the human soul, primordially constituted of the three principles just spoken of in due balance and proportion and divinely pronounced to be "very good," has deflected from that state. Its fall has been affected by the disproportioned, unbalanced, and, therefore, disorderly abuse of its inherent powers. Just as a man in a temper becomes temporarily unbalanced and liable to do what he would not in serene moments, the soul has utterly disorganized its nature. Of the three pillars that should support it, Wisdom (Gnosis) has fallen and become replaced by a flexible and shifting prop of speculative opinion. Strength (divine dynamic energy) has become exchanged for the frailty of the perishing flesh. Beauty, the god-like radiant form that should adorn and liken man to his Divine Creator, has become superseded by every ugliness of imperfection. Man is now a ruined temple, over which is written "Ichabod! Ichabod! the glory is departed!" Severed from conscious contact with his Vital and Immortal Principle, he is a prisoner to himself and his lower temporal nature. It remains for him to retrace his steps and rebuild his temple. He cannot continue as a bondslave to his self-made illusions and the attractions of "worldly possessions." He must become a free man and Mason, engaged in shaping himself into a living and precious stone for the cosmic temple of a regenerate Humanity unto which, when completed and dedicated, Deity will again enter and abide.

To be "installed in the chair of King Solomon," therefore, means in its true sense the reattainment of a Wisdom we have lost and the revival in ourselves of the Divine Life-Essence which is the basis of our being. With the reattainment of that Wisdom, all that is comprised in terms of Strength and Beauty will also be reattained, for the three pillars stand in eternal association and balance. Not to again realize it, not to revive the Divine Life-Essence, during our sojourn in this world, is to miss the opportunity which life in physical conditions provides. This is because the after-death state is one not of labor at this work, but of refreshment and rest, where no real progress is possible. Initiation was instituted to impart the science of its reattainment and lift the individual soul to a new life basis from which it could work out its salvation and develop its inherent powers along the true line of its destiny and evolution. But, as the Ancient Mysteries taught, the soul that never even begins this work in this world will not be able to begin it hereafter but will remain suspended in the more tenuous planes of this planet until it is once again indrawn into the vortex of generation by the ever-turning wheel of life. To quote Plato again, "those who instituted the Mysteries for us taught us that whosoever descended into Hades (the after-death state) uninitiated and without being a partaker in the Mysteries, will be plunged into mire and darkness, but whoever arrived there purified and initiated will dwell with the Gods." This teaching is reproduced in Masonry about the Master-Mason being "admitted to the assembly of the just made perfect." The implication being that those who have not reached that proficiency and are neither "just" (*i.e.*, rectified) nor perfected, will abide upon a lower level of post-mortem existence. For the levels of superphysical life are numerous—"in my Father's house are many mansions," or, literally, resting places—and they and their occupants graduated in hierarchical order according to their degree of fitness and spiritual eminence. The disordered modern world, with its perverse independent ideals of equality and uniformity, has lost all sense of the hierarchic principle, which, since it obtains in the higher world, ought to be reflected in this.

> "Order is Heaven's first law and, that confessed,
> Some are, and must be, greater than the rest."

But Masonry preserves the witness to this graduation and to the existence of separate tiers of life in the heaven-places in the symbolic distribution of its more advanced members. In the symbolic clothing worn by the members of various ranks, the observant student will perceive the intention to express the truth appropriately, thereby indicating it. The Masonic apron has been explained in an earlier paper as a figure of the soul's corporeality—the body (not to be confused with the gross physical body) that it wears and will display when it passes from this life. Its pure white is fringed in the case of junior brethren with a pale shade of that blue which, even in physical nature, is the color of the heavens. With seniors in the Grand Lodges, this has intensified to the deepest degree of that hue in correspondence with their theoretical spiritual development, while the gold lace adornments of the clothing emblematize what is referred to in the Psalmist's words, "The King's daughter (the soul) is all glorious within; her clothing is of wrought gold." For as the Life-Essence or Wisdom becomes increasingly "wrought" or substantialized in us, it becomes the objectified corporeality of the soul. In the Royal Arch, the Craft devotional blue is interested in red, the color of fire or spiritual ardor, and the blend results in purple, which, both in Earth and Heaven, is the prerogative of royalty. Thus, by their clothing, the members of Masonry emblematize the angels and archangels on earth and all the company of Heaven. Some are clothed with light as with a garment; others are ministers of flaming fire.

In a short paper such as this, our reference to the Ancient Mysteries is necessarily brief and has been restricted to the Greek Eleusinian system. Many others existed, and an extensive, though scattered, literature is available for those who would pursue the subject further in the direction of the Egyptian, Samothracian, Chaldean, Mithraic, Gnostic, and other systems. In their respective days and localities, they formed the authoritative centers of religion and philosophy, using those terms as but phases of an indivisible subject. Nowadays, it has become split up into many brands of theology and speculative philosophy, with little and often no possible connection. What the old writers made public about the Mysteries, of course, discreetly avoids descriptions of the deeper truths they imparted or of the actual processes of initiation. These must always remain a subject of secrecy, but by the perspicuous reader, enough can be found in their purposely obscure and metaphorical accounts to indicate what occurred and with what effect upon the candidate. Initiation, we have already said, is something that the masses are unfit to receive, even after long and rigorous preparation, and fewer are still competent to impart. It was an experience that a writer has said regarding the candidate, *Vel invenit sanctum, vel facit*—it either finds him holy or makes him so. Virgil's account in the sixth Æneid of the initiation of Æneas into Elysium (or the supernatural light), or that of Lucius (again a name signifying enlightenment) in the "Golden Ass" of Apuleius, when he was permitted to "see the sun at midnight," are instructive instances. Also, there was the exclamation of Clement of Alexandria, who had been received into the Gnostic school: "O truly sacred Mysteries! O pure Light! I am led by the light of the torch to the view of Heaven and of God. I become holy by initiation. The Lord Himself is the hierophant who, leading the candidate for initiation to the Light, seals him and presents him to the Father to be preserved forever. These are the celebrations of my Mysteries. If thou wilt, come and be thou also initiated, and thou shalt join in the dance with the angels around the uncreated, imperishable, and only true God, the Word of God joining in the strain!"

The Mysteries ended as public institutions in the sixth century, when political considerations prohibited them and the Roman government's teaching of secret doctrine and philosophy under Justinian, who aimed at inaugurating an official uniform state religion throughout its Empire. Subsequently, as the Roman Empire declined and broke up, the Roman Catholic Church emerged from it, which, as we know, has resolutely discountenanced any authority in religion and philosophy as a rival to her own and, at the same time, claimed supremacy and an over-riding jurisdiction in temporal matters also. For the Freemason, the result of that Church's conduct was instructive. When an authority upon matters wholly spiritual and belonging to a kingdom which is not of this world lays claim to temporal power and secular possessions, as the Roman Church has done and still does, it at once invalidates and neutralizes its spiritual qualifications. It becomes infected with the virus of "worldly possessions." It loads itself with the "money and metals" from which it is essential to keep divested. The result has been that what might have been, and was designed to be, the greatest spiritually educative force in the world's history has become a materialized institution, exercising an intellectual tyranny that has estranged the minds of millions from religion altogether. As Lot's wife is metaphorically said to have crystallized into a pillar of salt through turning back in desire to what she ought to have renounced altogether, so in trying to serve Mammon and God at the same time, the Roman Church has failed in both. As the result of the false steps and abuses of centuries, the world is today a chaos of disunited sects and popular religious teaching as materialistic as Masonry. It is a pity, for in its original design and practice, Christianity was intended to serve as a system of initiation upon a catholic or universal scale and to take over, supersede, and amplify all that previously was taught in a less productive way and to a more restricted public, in the Ancient Mysteries. It is impossible here to enter upon the fascinating questions involved in the transition from pre-Christian to Christian religion or to explain why and how the Christian Mysteries are the flowering of the earlier ones and transcend them. The two methods are identical in their central teachings, as in the philosophical method of life they demand. The differences between them are only due to amplification and formal expression. Christianity did not come to destroy but to fulfill and expand. That fulfillment and expansion resulted from an event of cosmic importance, which we speak of as The Incarnation. Because of that event, something had happened, affecting the very fabric of our planet and every aspect of the human family. What that something was and the nature of the change it wrought is too great and deep a theme to develop at this time. But to illustrate it by Masonic symbolism, it was an event that is the equivalent of and is represented by the transference of the Sacred Symbol of the Grand Geometrician of the Universe from the ceiling of the Lodge, where it is located in the elementary grades of the Craft, to the floor, where it is found in the Royal Arch Degree surrounded with flaming lights and every circumstance of reverence and sanctity. How many Masons are there in the Order today who recognize that, in this piece of symbolism, Masonry is giving affirmation and visual testimony to precisely the same fact as the churchman affirms when he recites in his Creed the words "He came down from heaven and was incarnate and was made man."

By a tacit and entirely unwarranted convention, the members of the Craft avoid mention in their lodges of the Christian Master and confine their scriptural readings and references almost exclusively to the Old Testament. The motive being no doubt due to a desire to observe the injunction as to refraining from religious discussion and to prevent offense on the part of brethren who may not be of the Christian faith. The motive is an entirely misguided one and is negated by the fact that the "Greater Light" upon which every member is obligated, and to which his earnest attention is recommended from the moment of his admission to the Order, is not only the Old Testament but the volume of the Sacred Law in its entirety. The New Testament is as essential to his instruction as the Old, not merely because of its moral teaching, but because it constitutes the record of the Mysteries in their supreme form and historic culmination. The Gospels themselves, like the Masonic degrees, are a record of preparation and illumination, leading up to the ordeal of death, followed by a rising from the dead and the attainment of a Mastership. They exhibit the process of initiation carried to the highest conceivable degree of attainment. The New Testament is full of passages in Masonic terminology. There is not a little irony in the failure of modern Masons to recognize its supreme importance and relevancy to their lodge proceedings and in the fact that, in so doing, they may be likening themselves to those builders of whom it is written that they rejected the chief Cornerstone. They would learn further that the Grand Master and Exemplar of Masonry, Hiram Abiff, is but a figure of the Great Master and Exemplar and Savior of the world, the Divine Architect by whom all things were made, without whom is nothing that hath been made, and whose life is the light of men. If, in the words of the Masonic hymn:

> "Hiram the architect
> Did all the Craft direct
> How they should build,"

It is equally true that the protagonist of the Christian Scriptures also taught universal humanity "how they should build." He reconstructs their fallen nature and that the method of such building involves the cross as its working tool and one which culminates in a death and a raising from the dead. And, of those who attain their initiation and mastership by that method, is it not further written there that they become of the household of God and built into a spiritual temple not made with hands, but eternal and in the heavens and of which "Jesus Christ is the chief cornerstone, in whom all the building, fitly framed together, groweth unto a holy temple built for an habitation of God?"

Neither the Ancient Mysteries nor Modern Masonry, their descendant, therefore, can be rightly viewed without reference to their relation to the Christian gospel, into which the pre-Christian schools became assumed. The line of succession and evolution from the former to the latter is direct and organic. Allowing for differences in time, place, and form of expression taught the same truths and inculcated the necessity for regeneration. In such a matter, there cannot be a diversity of doctrines. The truth concerning it must be static and uniform throughout world history. Hence, we find St. Augustine affirming that there has never existed but one religion in the world since the beginning of time (meaning by religion the science of rebinding the dislocated soul to its source) and that that religion began to be called Christian in apostolic times. And hence, too, it is that both the Roman Church and Masonry, although so widely divergent in outlook and method, have this feature in common that each declares and insists that no alteration or innovation in its central doctrine is permissible and that it is unlawful to remove or deviate from its ancient landmarks. Each is right in its insistence, for in the system of each is enshrined the age-old doctrine of regeneration and divinization of the human soul, obscured in one case by theological and other accretions foreign to the main purpose of religion and unperceived in the other because its symbolism remains uninterpreted. To clear vision, Christian and Masonic doctrines are identical in intention though different in method. The one says "*Via Crucis*"; the other says "*Via Lucis*," yet, the two ways are but one way. The former teaches through the ear, the latter through the eye, and by identifying the aspirant with the doctrine by passing him personally and dramatically through symbolic rites, which he is expected to translate from ceremonial form into subjective experience. As Patristical literature shows, the primitive method of the Christian Church was not that which now obtains, under which the religious offices and teaching are administered to the whole public alike and in a way implying a common level of doctrine for all and uniform power of comprehension by every member of the congregation. It was, on the other hand, a graduated method of instruction and identical with the Masonic system of degrees conferred because of advancing merit and ability. To cite one of the most instructive of early Christian treatises (Dionysius: *On the Ecclesiastical Hierarchy*), with which every Masonic student should familiarize himself, it will be found that admission to the early Church was by three ceremonial degrees exactly corresponding in intention with those of Masonry. "The most holy initiation of the Mystic Rites has as its first Godly purpose the holy cleansing of the initiated; and as second, the enlightening instruction of the purified; and finally, and as the completion of the former, the perfecting of those instructed in the science of their appropriate instructions. The order of the Ministers in the first class cleanses the initiated through the

Mystic Rites; in the second, conducts the purified to light; and, in the last and highest, makes perfect those who have participated in the Divine Light by the scientific contemplations of the illuminations contemplated." This brief passage alone shows that the Christian Church's original membership involved a sequence of three initiatory rites identical in intention to those of the Craft today. The names given to those who had qualified in those Rites were Catechumens, Leiturgoi, and Priests or Presbyters, which in turn are identifiable with our Entered Apprentices, Fellow Crafts, and Master Masons. Their first degree was that of rebirth and purification of the heart; their second related to the illumination of the intelligence; and their third to a total death unto sin and a new birth unto righteousness, in which the candidate died with Christ on the cross, as with us he is made to imitate the death of Hiram, and was raised to that higher order of life which is Mastership.

When Christianity became a state religion and the Church a world power, the materialization of its doctrine proceeded quickly and only increased with the centuries. Instead of becoming the unifying force its leaders meant it to be, its association with "worldly possessions" has made it a disintegrated one. At the same time, the Protestant communities and so-called "free" churches have unhappily become self-severed altogether from the original tradition. Their imagined liberty and independence are captivity to ideas of their own, having no relation to the primitive gnosis and no understanding of those Mysteries that must always lie deeper than the exoteric popular religion of a given period. Regeneration as a science has long been, and still is, entirely outside the purview of orthodox faith. The Christian Master's affirmation "Ye must be born again" is regarded as but a pious counsel towards an indefinite improvement of conduct and character, not as a reference to a drastic scientific revolution and reformation of the individual in the way contemplated by the rites of initiation prescribed in the Mysteries. Popular religion may produce "good" men, as the world's standard of goodness goes. But it does not and cannot produce divinized men endued with the qualities of Mastership, for it is ignorant of the traditional wisdom and methods by which that end is to be attained.

However, that wisdom and those traditional methods of the Mysteries have never been without living witness in the world, despite the jealousy and inhibitions of official orthodoxy. Since the suppression of the Mysteries in the sixth century, their tradition and teaching have been continued in secret and under various concealments, and to that continuation, our present Masonic system is due. As previously intimated in these papers, it was compiled and projected between two and three centuries ago as an elementary expression of the ancient doctrine and initiatory method by a group of minds that were far more deeply instructed in the old tradition and secret science than are those who avail themselves of their work today, or even than the text of the Masonic rites indicates. Suppose they remained obscure and anonymous, so the modern student's research cannot identify them. In that case, it is only what is to be expected, for the true initiate is one who never proclaims himself as such and is content ever to remain impersonal and out of sight and notoriety, planting his seed for the welfare of his fellow men indifferently and leaving others to water it and God to give it increase. But, within the limits they allowed themselves, they achieved their work well and truly made it a revision, faithful at least in outline and main principles, of the ancient teaching and perfecting rites of the philosophic Mysteries. It has been well said by a writer of authority on the subject that they put forward the system of speculative Masonry as "an experiment upon the mind of the age" and to exhibit to at least a small section of the public living in a time of gross darkness and materialism. If this theory is true, their intention may, at first sight, have become falsified by subsequent developments.

During what has sprung up as an organization of worldwide dimensions and vast membership, animated by worthy ideals and accomplishing a certain measure of benevolent work, the original purpose of this Order for promoting the science of human regeneration seemed to have become lost. A broader and wiser view of the situation would be that, while recognizing a great diffusion of energy to little present purpose, we also see that the effort is not wasted but conserved. We see that, besides benefiting individuals here and there who are capable of truly profiting from the Order, it preserves the witness and keeps burning the light of the perpetual Mysteries in a dark age. Like the Light of a Master Mason, which never becomes wholly extinguished, so in the world's darkest days, the Light of the Mysteries never goes out entirely. God and the way to Him are not left without witness. If, in comparison with other witnesses, Masonry is but a glimmering ray rather than a powerful beam of light, it is nonetheless a true ray, a kindly Light lit from the world's Central Altar flame and sufficing to lead at least some of us on amid the encircling gloom, until the night is gone. Light is granted in proportion to the desire of our hearts, but for most Masons, their Order sheds no Light at all because Light is not their desire. Nor is initiation in its true sense understood or wished for. They move among the symbols, representations, and substituted secrets of the Mysteries without comprehending them, without wanting to translate them into reality. The Craft is made to subserve social and philanthropic ends foreign to its purpose and even to gratify the desire for outward personal distinction. Still, as an instrument of regeneration, it remains wholly ineffective.

Is this unknowingness, this unreceptiveness and failure to comprehend, however, to no purpose? Perhaps not. Each of us lives in the presence of natural mysteries he fails to discern or understand, and even when the desire for wisdom is at last awakened, education is a long process. Nature in all her kingdoms builds slowly, perfecting her aims through endless repetitions and wanton waste of material. And in the things of the Kingdom that transcend Nature, the same method prevails. Souls are drawn but slowly to the Light, and their perfecting and transmutation into that Light is often very gradual. For a long time, before it can distinguish shadow from substance, humanity must try its prentice-hand upon illusory toys and substitutions for the genuine secrets of reality. For long before it is worthy of initiation upon the path that leads to God, it must be permitted to indulge in preliminary unintelligent rehearsals of the processes involved. The approaches to the ancient temples of the Mysteries were lined with statues of the Gods, having no value of themselves but intended to habituate the minds of neophytes to the spiritual concepts and divine attributes to which those statues were meant to give objective form and semblance. But within the temple itself, all graven images, all formal figures, symbols, and ceremonial types, ceased, for the mind had then finally learned to dispense with their help and, in the strength of its own purity and understanding alone, to rise into the unclouded perception of their formless prototypes and "see the Nameless of the hundred names."

"Get knowledge, get wisdom; but with all thy gettings, get understanding," exclaims the old Teacher, in a counsel that may well be commended to the Masonic Fraternity today, which understands so little its system. But understanding depends upon the gift of the Supernal Light, which gift, in turn, relies on the zeal of our desire for it. If Wisdom today is widowed, all Masons are, or potentially, the widow's sons. She will be justified by the children who seek her out and labor for her as a hidden treasure. It remains with the Craft itself whether it shall enter upon its heritage as a lineal successor of the Ancient Mysteries and Wisdom-teaching or whether, by failing so to do, it will undergo the inevitable fate of everything that is but a form from which its native spirit has departed.

146

Virtus Junxit, Mors Non Separabit

Thank you for buying this Cornerstone book!

For over 25 years now, we've tried to provide the
Masonic community with quality books on
Masonic education, philosophy, and general interest.
Your support means everything to us and
keeps us afloat. Cornerstone is by no means a large
company. We are a small family owned operation
that depends on your support.

Please visit our website and have a look at the
many books we offer as well as the different
categories of books.

If your lodge, Grand Lodge, research lodge, book
club, or other body would like to have quality
Cornerstone books to sell or distribute, write us. We
can give you outstanding books, prices, and service.

Thanks again!